"Tina is a seeker… ⟨illegible⟩ …in her writing and her life. Going on this journey with her will not be a straight path with all the answers, but an adventure; with Tina as your guide."

—*Kemi Nekvapil, author of* Power: A woman's guide to living and leading without apology

"Tina travels within words, through time and space, to give voice to the most challenging moments, the victories, the vitality of breathing deeply. Charming, useful, real and moving."

—*Elena Brower, bestselling author and host of the* Practice You Podcast

"Tina, through her own absolute honesty, encourages readers to be equally honest with themselves. Merging visceral storytelling, ancient wisdom, and practical guidance—watch out. This daring book causes emotional and spiritual breakthroughs. Your life might not be the same after reading it."

—*Dr Bella Ellwood-Clayton, author of* Weekend Friends *and* Sex Drive

BIG little *breath*

BIG
little
breath

A TRAVEL GUIDE *for* **YOUR SPIRIT**

TINA BRUCE

First published by the kind press, 2024
Copyright © Tina Bruce, 2024

The moral right of the author has been asserted.
All rights reserved. No part of this publication may be reproduced, published, performed in public or communicated to the public in any form or by any means without prior written permission from The Kind Press. Every effort has been made to trace creators and copyright holders of quoted material included in this book. The publisher welcomes hearing from anyone not correctly acknowledged.

Cover artwork and illustrations by Hannah Sutton, Artist
Author images by Prue Aja, Photography
Print information available on the last page.
A catalogue record for this book is available from the National Library of Australia.
ISBN: 978-0-6458656-9-1 paperback
ISBN: 978-0-6458656-8-4 (eBook)

THE KIND PRESS

thekindpress.com

We at The Kind Press acknowledge that Aboriginal and Torres Strait Islander peoples are the Traditional Custodians and the first storytellers of the lands on which we live and work; and we pay our respects to Elders past and present.

This book is part memoir. All of the events are true to the best of the author's memory. Some names and identifying features have been changed to protect the identity of certain parties. It is sold with the understanding that the author and publisher are not engaged in rendering advice or any kind of personal or professional service in the book. In the event that you use any of the information in this book for yourself, the author and the publisher assume no responsibility for your actions. Please check with a medical professional before embarking on any breathwork practice.

This book is dedicated to—
All creatures great and small
Especially for Leila and Zoë

Contents

A Note From The Author — xi
Foreword — xiii
Introduction: This Is Not A Spiritual Book — xvii

Part I

Chapter 1   Cracked Mirrors — 1
Chapter 2   Charming Children — 25
Chapter 3   21 Days In The Desert — 43
Chapter 4   Alcohol Is Not Ruining My Life But I Can't Stop Drinking — 71
Chapter 5   Surf Indo Waves — 89
Chapter 6   Stories Of A White Privileged Woman — 105

Part II

Chapter 7   Midlife Mountain — 121
Chapter 8   Let Go Of Control — 137
Chapter 9   Be A People Disappointer — 153
Chapter 10   Himalayan Heartwork — 167
Chapter 11   Take Risks — 189
Chapter 12   Medusa Jellyfish — 207
Chapter 13   Don't Die Trying — 221

Epilogue — 238
Acknowledgements — 240
About The Author — 242

A NOTE FROM THE AUTHOR

This book is a memoir. In telling my stories, I have included scenes, descriptions and conversations with others that are not intended to be word-for-word re-enactments. They reflect my recollections and interpretations. Some names have been changed to protect the privacy of individuals and some events have been dramatised for the sake of the narrative. I want to emphasise that this book contains information about my personal journey, including lessons learned along the way, and is no way intended to be a substitute for medical advice or therapy.

FORWORD

Dr Ricci-Jane Adams, author of *Spiritually Fierce* and *Superconscious Intuition*

Tina Bruce is a woman who leaves a lasting impression. When she embarked on her studies with the Institute for Intuitive Intelligence, I was intrigued. What could this confident, independent thinker be seeking from further exploration of intuition? It quickly became apparent that Tina was not just a student but a leader in her own right. She was already in the process of writing her first book, *Mother's Medicine*, and was actively involved in her community, making a positive impact on the world around her.

Tina is striking. Tall, beautiful and magnetic, she lights up every room she enters. As I came to know Tina more through her time with the Institute, I understood a deeper, richer truth about this woman. Yes, she is an independent thought leader, clear in her own ideas and confident in bringing them to the world. She is also a humble seeker, a woman of paradox, who inspires other women to deeper truths within themselves whilst she wrestles with her own shadows alongside them. She doesn't claim to have it all together, and she bravely shares her story and evolution with others. Tina walks her talk. She could be written off as a beautiful, privileged well-being influencer, but that would betray a richer truth.

In her first book, Tina shared her story of recovering from opioid addiction by reconnecting to her intuition - her inner wisest self. *Mother's Medicine* is one of the bravest books I have read. It is a breathtaking read, and yet, I believe that *Big Little Breath* is even more compelling. Tina's power as a writer is that she holds nothing back. *Mother's Medicine* is a no-holds-barred account of the darkest parts of herself. In her latest book, Tina gives us her exact recipe for participatory and vulnerable leadership. She gives us all the wisdom she has attained as a life-long student and powerhouse teacher of truth. She doesn't conceal the formula, offering only the highlights and asking that you spend more money or time with her to get the specifics. Tina generously lays it all out for our empowerment.

Like all great teachers, Tina's highest goal is service. In this case through the transmission of the Intuitive Mountain Map, a specific, precise and tested approach to increasing access to our own intuition. Tina is in this life to invite us to access the greatest parts of ourselves and gives us her map without hesitation. It is a map created by walking the path when there was no path. What we have the privilege of absorbing from the comfort of our homes has been crafted from Tina's embodied experience of rising in the pre-dawn darkness, hundreds of hours of devotion, leaping into the unknown, vanquishing inner demons and generally living outside of her comfort zone for extended periods of time (or perhaps her whole life). Tina's sweat, tears and tireless effort are now eloquently offered on these pages.

Tina is not afraid of entering the underbelly of human experience. I have watched her navigate socially conscious leadership, dismantling her own white privilege, and understanding indigenous experience to the best of her ability, while others have stayed hidden in the comfort of the Western, white-centric spiritual and well-being industry, benefiting from their privilege without questioning it. She has humbled herself time and again, and even in her missteps, she has not scurried back to the comfort of the spaces that tell her she doesn't have to try that hard. Tina is authenticity itself. It is not easy to live this way. It is often lonely and isolating; To embody new paradigm leadership is to break new ground, to shatter the mould, to stay in the fire. The authentic leader, the spiritful leader, to use Tina's term, is an agitator and a disruptor. There is no one around you who can confirm that you are on the right path because you are creating the path.

In the fullness of time, I have come to know that what I can offer this brave and audacious leader is respite, a safe harbour to dock from time to time to renew her capacity to change the world. It has been my absolute privilege to do this. Tina never needed me to show her the way. As we learn in *Big Little Breath,* she has been making her own way all her life. Motivated by an inner fire for the authentic, I have no fear that Tina will ever lose her way. She is the demonstration of all that she offers. The world is better for her being in it and for the generous blessing of this book.

I devoured *Big Little Breath* in a day. I know that you will also find this book to be a page-turner. I encourage you not just to be absorbed by the compelling personal stories but to give yourself over to the practices and processes so generously offered. Let this book alter you. We, as the readers, have the easy part. Tina is offering us the gold of her lived experience on a platter. Make the most of it. Sink into it all. Read it and read it again. And then embody the wisdom. You will be richly rewarded for humbly showing up to this profound guidebook to the deepest states of intuition.

Dr Ricci-Jane Adams
Principal of the Institute for Intuitive Intelligence
April 2024

INTRODUCTION

THIS IS NOT A SPIRITUAL BOOK

"We find that, all along, we had what we needed from the beginning and that in the end we have returned to its essence, an essence we could not understand until we had undertaken the journey."
—David Whyte

This is not a spiritual book. This is a spiritful book.
The following story is about my exploration into becoming Spiritful.

Spiritful, according to the Merriam-Webster definition, means full of spirit or vigour, animated, spirited, vigorous. A charming creature.
Spiritual means relating to people's thoughts and beliefs, rather than to their bodies, energy and physical surroundings.

Since publishing my last book, *"Mother's Medicine: the birth of my intuition"*, I've been on a continuing journey of self-discovery which was 'spiritful' more than 'spiritual' or 'religious'. What I've learned is that we do not need more spiritual people. Spirituality is dependent on one's beliefs, opinions and personal experiences.

The word spirit originates from the Latin root *spiritus*, which means *breath*.

To be spiritful means to be full of breath, energy and life. Being spiritful feels more expansive. To be a seeker of our own spirit and not somebody else's meandering search for meaning and purpose. It transcends our separate self completely. The lower mind self that gets in the way of our own full inhale and exhale and connection with the soul and our truest expression.

Spirit is not the private property of any belief system or opinionated group. The moment you attach to a belief, you invite a certain rigidity or anchor into the field of awareness that you are. This book is for spiritual leaders, not spiritual gurus. As a spiritual person, I have no doctrine to propagate, no philosophies to preach, no agenda to push upon. This is because there is only one way for you to evolve towards wholeness and that is for you to fall in love with your own charming creature and follow your intuition. I have found that most people want a path that is free of dogma and die-hard rules. A path that is simple and does not need to be practised in churches, ashrams or monasteries, but can be included anywhere and within their own bodies.

Evolving a global village of human beings who are creative, flexible and open to being curious towards others, rather than stuck in their ways, shapes a different kind of culture. Can you imagine it? During the epoch of living through a pandemic in the most locked down city in the world at one stage, Melbourne, Australia, I was shocked to discover that my spiritual practices stopped working. What happened to the yoga, the meditation, the breathwork, the mantras, the intuition?

Everything was challenged, including my beliefs about the world. My energy levels became loaded with an unnamed heaviness. The leaders I looked up to no longer inspired me. Creative flow dried up, and my ability to trust myself was on the edge. Little did I know at the time that 'the edge' is where all the magic happens. It's not easy to be alive peacefully when the outside world wants to rage on. The anxiety of living makes us judge, be sure, have a stance, definitively decide. Let's face it, it's traumatic to be a human being in a body, let alone keeping an open loving heart that includes all beings from all backgrounds. Having a fixed, rigid spiritual system of belief can therefore be a great relief and offer us a sense of belonging. But it comes at a cost. We never seem to tire of wanting to tell others what to believe, how to believe, and even at what hours of the day or week they should practise those beliefs.

Being continually told who we 'should be', we end up borrowing other people's beliefs, and become influenced, and worse, programmed by their fears and limitations. Opinion is really the lowest form of knowledge because it requires no truth. Intuition is the highest form of knowledge because it comes from a pure place. Carl Jung, Jungian psychologist, describes this phenomenon as the 'collective unconscious.' He coined the term to signify the beliefs we hold that are based on what others have taught us. All these beliefs are centred around seeking answers externally and accepting other's ideas of how life should be.

Like a psychic sponge, I had absorbed so many noisy opinions and different beliefs from the collective soup it cost me my authentic voice. This happened very sneakily without me even realising it. On the journey to be seen to be doing the right thing and pleasing everyone, I lost myself. I needed to find myself again without the external voices. No one else in the world knew what was best for me, not my family, the experts, the teachers, my mates, because none of these people had ever lived my experiences, breathed in my body, slept in my skin.

I longed to be filled up with spirit and aliveness. I wasn't looking for more judgements or justifications. I was looking for the charm and to be filled with truthful essence again. To bridge the gap between suffering and the place we can become most estranged from—our creative dancing spirits.

I wondered what happened to my spiritful charming creature?

This book is divided into two parts. The first is the 'what' and the second is the 'how'. **Part 1** describes the charming creature in all its forms and **Part 2** offers you a way to find it. The framework for *The Intuitive Mountain Map* in **Part 2** is based on transcending seven fears.

The seven fear issues are all related to seven energy centres of our body known as chakras. These fears are energetically located in our flesh and bones based on frequency and vibration.

Every attachment or traumatic memory we hold on to out of fear demands some portion of our spirit to leave our energy field, which eventually leads to contraction and dis-ease in our cell tissue. Over time, this causes us to lose our charm and our ability to discern between the true voice within and the scared voice of the ego. Trauma left unprocessed makes us believe we are not deserving of more in our life. It convinces us that settling is the answer. To be in collusion with this false self is to believe the lie of wounded ego consciousness. This is the precursor to us losing our charm and not listening to our intuition. People find it easy to say that they are intuitive. They like to tune in and connect to their intuitive powers when it is convenient or when they're in crisis and desperate for guidance. In other words, they like to control their intuition on a part time basis when it suits them.

What people find challenging is actually living their intuition full time. Is that even possible? To live in alignment with your heart and mind, to walk your talk, to be the embodiment of a prophet in action? People know the truth that is steering them in a certain direction but struggle to act on the truth. Most of our choices either default to running on autopilot or we stay the same, accept lower standards for ourselves and repeat the decisions that are familiar and comfortable for us.

The real reason people don't live their intuition fully is because they are still re-living their trauma. The fears that have made a home in their bodies block their intuition.

Every single human knows what it's like to be consumed by fear or may have even spent some serious time through a dark night of the soul. Every one of us has not listened to our intuition and fucked up as a result. I've not always been living my best life, and this means I'm just like you.

The great philosopher Rumi refers to this predicament as 'the open secret'. It's a laughable admission that we're all hiding the exact same story. Just like you, I sometimes do unkind and cowardly things towards myself and others. I'm ashamed of how I react when I'm feeling insecure or jealous. I worry over the stuff I can't control. And I blame my past for all the traumatic events that should never have happened to me! In Nietzsche's memorable phrase, 'human, all too human', we're all just as flawed and imperfect as each other. The difference is whether we repeat the same patterns, or whether we learn, heal and evolve through it?

The definition of trauma I have based this story around is from medical intuitive Caroline Myss who states, 'What traumatises us is any experience that shatters our capacity to reason our way through it. Anything that shatters our sense of trust, justice and our feeling that we can protect ourselves from the unknown. The core of your trauma is that your survival instincts get shattered in a way you can't even articulate.'

Big 'T's are distressing or 'shattering' events that fall beyond the scope of normal human experience and are most commonly associated with PTSD (post-traumatic stress disorder). Big T trauma that has not been processed or stays stuck in the nervous system causes one of the altered states known as 'The Four Fs' that make up the trauma response—fight, flight, freeze and fawn. Until these nervous responses are regulated again, Big T trauma will have the loudest voice in your system and will internally turn you against yourself out of fear for your survival.

For me, this eventually led to chronic pain and a serious addiction to opioid prescription painkillers that dominated my life for many years. Research has shown that all forms of trauma have a strong correlation with substance abuse. Numbing the emotional triggers feels like the only option in order to function as a member of society. After much investment in my health and allowing years to heal body, mind, spirit and soul, the quality of my life improved dramatically until personal growth invited more layers to the surface to be seen. Many people believe that the traumas in our life are a one-time experience. However, there are also less obvious little 't' traumas that often go unacknowledged. They can snowball over the course of an adult life. The last few years have been a confrontation with the little 't' traumas which have been much more subtle but perhaps even more powerful in blocking my intuition and making me afraid of situations and people where there was no real threat.

Little 't's include non-life-threatening incidents such as emotional abuse, bullying, harassment, death of a pet, divorce, infidelity, loss of a job or career, illness, generational traumas and many more. It can also be as subtle as the tone or manner somebody repeatedly speaks to you if it feels diminishing or condescending. Interestingly, many of our little 't's occur during childhood when we are under-resourced emotionally at the time to process and cope with relationship dynamics, powers of discernment and decision making. When you have been on a spiritual journey or personal growth journey for many years, eventually your subconscious pushes these experiences up into the conscious mind to be healed.

About eleven Tina's ago in 2018, I wrote a book called *"Mother's Medicine, the birth of my intuition"*, which tells my story of how I was addicted and chronically in pain due to the birth trauma of my first-born child. Since I published this book, the story of moving through trauma and addiction has surprisingly continued. Once I let go of the strong painkiller drug dependence, other addictions took their place—more culturally accepted ones such as alcohol, social media, work and co-dependent relationships. All served their purpose to numb emotional discomfort and control the outside world.

At the root of all this behaviour was more trauma. A whole moving carousel of different-sized baggage circled around me. The Universe witnessed and waited to see which suitcase I'd grab next to unpack. Once I emptied the 'Big T' special oversized bag from the 'heavy items only' counter, lots of 'Little T' carry-ons followed. Each one was full of childhood fears, accumulated from past travel and lost in the wrong hands of various baggage handlers. It was time to take ownership and reclaim this luggage as I tried to make meaning out of the chaos of myself and the world around me.

Healing from the birth of my first child was an event that could be considered a Big T trauma. Experiencing surgery without anaesthetic is akin to torture. Wars, natural disasters, pandemics, physical, racist and sexual abuse, witnessing death and experiencing harm and neglect would also fall into this category. This trauma led to a three to four yearlong caterpillar phase where I became unrecognisable to myself. My addict kept the prescription opioid pills in a zip lock sandwich bag next to my toddlers' snacks while I dragged them from clinic to pharmacy 'doctor shopping' for the next script. I came to depend on the drugs for a chronic nerve pain condition. I came to depend on the drugs emotionally as well as physically. I came to depend on the drugs to help me deal with having two small children as well as working part time in a demanding industry. I came to realise I had two massive problems. The trauma at the root of all of this pain which I had suppressed, and the trauma of the addiction layered on top, knowing there was a good chance it could kill me. As a parent, I didn't have the luxury of despair and collapse, so I kept pushing on with the pill pursuit.

I was soon caught, shamed and banned from my local GP for 'doctor shopping'. My first instinct was to lie and deny this accusation to my doctor out of fear she would cut off my supply. I lied, and she cut off my supply anyway. The next night, I woke up gasping for breath after taking too many pills the night before. It was either die of overdose or learn another way to manage chronic pain. I turned towards meditation like my life depended on it. Sitting for up to two hours at a time, I discovered my breath and body could create the chemistry and natural opiates far more powerfully than any drug or plant medicine. I heard my intuition say *you have everything you need to heal inside of you*. And yes, antidepressants also played an essential role during this phase, too.

I then went through intense opiate withdrawal which was not unlike a psychotic purging exorcism. But I survived it. I look back at my caterpillar now with so much gratitude for the work she did in the cocoon facing the trauma she desperately numbed. The caterpillar faced the fear and then set me free with new winged spiritual resources. It's a scientific fact that a butterfly has cellular memory of being in the cocoon. The physical form is where trauma is stored, but also where it's transformed. So, although the butterfly is renowned for being the charming creature in any metamorphosis, it's really a team effort. Caterpillars are also charming.

The only way out of a cocoon is to grow out of it.

This book picks up where *"Mother's Medicine"* left off pre-pandemic and is about how I navigated the little 't' fears that kept me stuck in people pleasing, perfectionism and productivity patterns of anxiety and self-doubt.

Getting to know my little 't's caused me to get closer to my little 'tina'.

Doing this inner child work was confronting, mainly because I discovered there was more than one little tina. I had a group of inner children who were scared, controlling, wounded and angry. Not one inner child but many! They all wanted the same thing, though—a more loving and trusting relationship with me now, as a forty-four-year-old woman. They wanted to know they could count on the inner intuitive adult to stand up for herself, make healthy choices and not need external validation.

By the end of this book, you will be able to identify your inner children, know the difference between the different kinds of intuition, and be empowered to live a life that is true, charming and authentic.

In writing this story, my intention is that you will no longer be afraid of your own life. I am hopeful that you, too, can see fear as not something to reject or be ashamed of, but as a doorway to living your intuition and finding your unique charming creature.

At the beginning of each chapter, I share parts of my story, some from my childhood, and some more current. You may see yourself in these stories, too, and they may help you feel less alone instead of internalising the traumas and burying them. Honour yourself for all the ways you have adapted and survived one hundred percent of your worst days.

Throughout this book, I also share the breathwork practices that supported me through becoming spirit *full*. Each practice enhances the seven ways of navigating your *Intuitive Mountain* so that you have a road map, especially for those days when you can't find your charming creature.

Breath is connected to freedom from fear. When people are afraid, they hold their breath. When they trust, they breathe with ease. Breathwork is a powerful practice to clear the subconscious where the body keeps the score and clears the noise in our heads so we can feel lighter and more present. It's also the thread that regulates our nervous systems and connects us with divine consciousness and intuition.

I have helped thousands of people through breathwork to regulate their nervous systems, release trauma and grief from their bodies, and access spiritual connections previously lost or buried under unconscious fears. However, it's important to note that the tools in this book are not the solution to your freedom. The breath is not a technique to be perfected. It's largely a mystery of consciousness which we are not meant to solve. I hope you're opening your mind now to all sorts of possibilities. When we oxygenate our life with breath, possibility, light and sound, our power can find its way into new spaces. We may even learn to like and appreciate our challenges. Overall, the breath asks us to live the questions *Who am I?* and *Why was I even born?*

It's really about the person you are being when you're not practicing or in devotion on the mat, and your unique charm energy which will touch the hearts of all who cross your path.

I would like to bring to attention that I am not a medical doctor or trauma therapist. My scope of practice is working with trauma-informed modalities, including *Medical Intuition, Rebirthing Breathwork, Yoga* and *Spinal Energetics*. I am inspired by the works of Dr Caroline Myss, Dr Bessel Van der Kolk and Dr Gabor Mate, based around how the body keeps the score and the healing power of the soul. I also want to acknowledge that I write from a place of white privilege. There will be blind spots and racial biases in this book which I'm actively working to dismantle and unlearn so I can support others from diverse backgrounds in healing collectively. I am a work-in-progress and apologise if anything comes across as ignorant or not inclusive. I would be grateful for any feedback where I can improve.

Your original charm is the true presence of your energy before conditioning or societal rules blanketed the freedom of your birthright to the great mystery of intuition.

> Your charming creature can be free and doesn't need to be hidden inside. I invite you now to take a deep inhale.
> Our breath marks the beginning of our journey together.
> Let's call your spirit home.

―――――――――――――――

"Midlife is when the universe gently places her hands upon your shoulders, pulls you close, and whispers in your ear: I'm not screwing around. All of this pretending and performing—these coping mechanisms that you've developed to protect yourself from feeling inadequate and getting hurt—has to go. Your armour is preventing you from growing into your gifts. I understand that you needed these protections when you were small.
I understand that you believed your armour could help you secure all of the things you needed to feel worthy and loveable, but you're still searching and you're more lost than ever. Time is growing short. There are unexplored adventures ahead of you. You were born worthy of love and belonging. You were made to live and love with your whole heart. It's time to show up and be seen."

—Brené Brown

―――――――――――――――

Part I

CHAPTER 1
CRACKED MIRRORS

"Conscious parenting is the parent who dares to raise themselves first. Who looks at the dynamic they have with their children as a mirror for all their unresolved baggage."

—Dr Shefali

I board the bus and don't know any of the year seven students from the other schools. I sit alone and stare out the window while listening to high-pitched voices chattering and squealing. After two hours, we arrive at music camp somewhere near the Gold Coast, a place called Tallebudgera. Designated to a dorm with about ten other girls, I watch them all run to grab their preferred bunkbed and sleeping arrangements. The last bed is on the bottom bunk near the toilet, and I walk over to place my backpack down on top of it. Crawling inside to lie on the hard, smelly mattress, I notice my tummy rumbling and wonder when we'll get to eat.

"Hey, you," a voice shouts from above me.

I tilt my head to the side and look up.

"Hi, I'm Mikaela. Looks like we're sharing a bunk together," she says, smiling.

Relieved to have met someone, I smile back hopefully and say, "Hi,

I'm Tina. I play the clarinet. What do you play?"

Suddenly, the room goes quiet and I hear whispering as all the other faces turn towards us.

Mikaela says, "Oh, umm, I play the violin. Stick your head out and look up at me so I can see you properly."

I move my body side-on to the mattress and hang my head over so our eyes lock and we can squarely see each other.

Sluuuuurp, pfffft, Mikaela snorts and makes a harking, throaty sound.

Directly above me, a big dollop of saliva is dripping from her mouth as I watch it in slow motion bungee jump from her lips, and within seconds, land splat on my nose.

Laughter erupts throughout the cabin as I realise what's just happened. A hot wave of humiliation washes up my head and my skin turns bright red. Spit is dripping down my cheeks and I wait for my tears to spill over, but they don't. I wipe away her saliva with my hands and wish the stinky mattress would swallow me whole, so I disappear. I get up silently to go to the bathroom instead.

"Aww, sorry, that was an accident," she yells out to me as the snickering continues.

Looking at my reflection in the mirror, I splash my face with water and wonder how I'll survive the next three days. A voice of authority booms over the chaos and laughter.

"Girls! Sneakers on. You are to be ready for our sport session in five minutes," the male teacher shouts.

I breathe a sigh of relief that I have a job to do and get my shoes on while avoiding eye contact with anyone. We are told to run five kilometres up the beach without stopping. As fifty children start jogging, I charge forwards and let my legs carry me away from the shame and the embarrassment. I enjoy the sensation of pushing myself away from fear and replacing it with physical pain instead. Huffing and puffing, I keep going all the way to the end, dedicated to obeying the task like a good girl.

After our run, we are told to head into the canteen for dinner. There, grey-looking meat and soggy vegetables sit in bright fluoro-yellow macaroni cheese. I take a small bread roll and leave the rest. Each morning and night, we repeat this running routine before and after we practise our musical instruments and group rehearsals. The more time is taken up with activities, the less I need to face unstructured and dangerous social time. I volunteer to clean up after meals while not eating anything except bread rolls for three days.

Exhausted and homesick, I shuffle onto the bus to return to town with the rest of the children. Mikaela is distributing lollies and handing out prizes for her 'best friends' while I sit in my baggier clothes and put my clarinet case beside me on the spare seat. I believe that this feeling of starvation, emptiness and invisibility is a superpower. Nobody will notice a thing. Nobody will see me.

"This is very serious, Tina. You have anorexia nervosa. Children die from this disease. If you don't put on one kilogram of weight by next week, I'll admit you to hospital. You'll be fed through a drip. You won't like it," Dr Patrick says sternly, peering through his thick brown rimmed glasses.

I look back at Dr Patrick with wide hollow eyes. My face is gaunt and grey, and I shrink even further into nothing as a spotlight shines on my shame. My mother sitting next to me is fragile and broken after divorcing my father. She adjusts her bag on her lap and waits for my reaction.

"Ok, I'll try," I reply.

"I'll try," I say again to be more convincing. I'm becoming good at lying as I learn to protect my invisibility. Trying is lying.

I am eleven years old, and I just want everyone to leave me alone.

Really, everything's been great the last few months as I've shrunk to half my body size. Being invisible is a superpower. I don't bother anyone. They don't bother me. It's like I don't exist at all and can evaporate like the wind back into the sky. I don't want to be seen. You can't lose people who can't even find you in the first place. It's so much safer this way. Being unseen is the answer.

Driving home from the doctor's office, I sit in the passenger seat. Thoughts are swirling through my brain. The last thing I want is to go to hospital where I can no longer control what goes into my body. Medicine, IV tubes, fluids, calories crawling under the unsealed doors like gremlins attacking me through bare skin. Anorexia captures me. Terrified and tied up, the doctor's fear-based strategy makes me even more ashamed of eating.

When we arrive home, my mum walks straight into the kitchen to follow through on her plan to fatten me up. The blender comes out and my worst nightmare goes in. Full cream milk, vanilla ice cream, chocolate, and banana.

Whizzzzzzzzzzz. The loud whirring of the blades fades as she slams the thick liquid concoction down on the table with determination.

Pouring it boldly, she pleads with me to drink the milkshake.

"C'mon Tina, just have half of it and that will be enough. Please try!" she begs.

We sit at the kitchen bench for what feels like hours staring at this glass filled with fat. I can't let it near my mouth. We sit in silence and the great stare off continues, waiting to see who will draw a breath first. All I want is to be left alone, except now I'm under surveillance and this is not going to happen. I can't tip the drink down the sink and pretend I had it with her eyes on me. This is war and all of my defences are on alert.

With shaky hands, I lift the glass to my lips and shudder at the smell of sweetness. I'm making calculations in my head around how long I'll need to exercise to burn it off. I drink about three sips and feel immediately concretised, guilty and heavy.

"There, I did it," I say defiantly.

"I'm going for a run," I declare.

I put my sneakers on straightaway and head outside. Great, I'm in control again. I really like the feeling of running away from something. Sometimes, I imagine a tiger is chasing me, so I go faster and burn more calories. My thirty-kilogram frame is not built for speed. It's running on air, the two pieces of apple I had for breakfast, and now the three sips of poison. A memory flashes back from music camp when I ran furiously away from myself.

"Life is a mirror that gives back as much as it receives."
—Evan Connell

My first-born daughter is eleven and she looks like she is fading away instead of filling out. After being interstate for work, I arrive home and dump my suitcase in the hallway. In the past, I would hear the pitter patter sound of little feet running to greet me and feel the wrapping soft arms around my legs. This time is different. I can sense the vibration of feet moving but receive no welcome home party. Walking into the living room, I see Leila waving her arms at me, but she's preoccupied with what's happening on the screen.

Watching her jump up and down in front of the television to a YouTube video instantly triggers panic inside my guts. In the year 1990, it was a VHS tape playing either Jane Fonda or Aerobics Oz Style. I burned through that tape daily, hitting play every single morning like a religious ritual. I burned through calories, ensuring the numbers game worked in my favour. I burned through any cravings for sugar or nourishment so I could stay comfortably empty. I burned through puberty so I could avoid it completely.

"Hi," I smile. "Can I get a hug?"

"As soon as I finish this, Mum," she pants.

After two hundred and ninety days of Melbourne lockdown, Leila repeats a fixed routine. It's like the cage door has flung wide open but the parrot is staying put, firm on her perch, or rather, forcing the effort to bounce enough on the one spot until her cheeks flush and sweat beads. Tamed into control, her wings have been clipped and the sky has been forgotten.

I remember that I've stashed some banana bread in my handbag and offer it to her as a snack. I'm desperate to see her actually put some food in her mouth, like a mother bird trying to force a meal down her baby's throat with her beak. I leave it on the bench and ask her to eat it as soon as she's finished.

Later, I find the banana bread hidden in the back of the pantry, shoved out of sight. My heart starts thumping in my chest. Hiding food is like a game of chess, strategically moving it around until challenged by your opponent. A memory flashes through my brain of when I threw the roast lamb off my dinner plate and under the stairs of the house. I would do this while walking from the kitchen to the downstairs rumpus room. Eventually you get found out. Either by the rats you are feeding underground or your family members.

"Leila, why did you hide the banana bread?" I confront her.

"I'm not hungry."

Our secrets live in the hiding. Our shame thrives in the secrets. Our potential to heal hides in the shame.

I'm too stunned to dig any deeper and we need to get to Saturday sport on time.

Watching her play, I notice how tiny she is compared to the other girls in her team. Taller but tiny. I tell myself it's because she's a whole year younger in age than everyone else in her grade.

It isn't until Leila's clothes begin to hang on her bony frame like old curtains that I begin to wonder what is going on.

Illness? Leukemia? Growth spurt? Early onset eating disorder?

Other parents glance at me, concern on their faces.

A friend approaches and asks, "Is Leila ok? She's lost so much weight. Has she been sick?"

For the first time, I say out loud, "She's not ok. I'm really worried. I need to do something."

Hearing my own voice shakes me out of denial and motivates me into action.

Driving home in the car we chat about the game and the win, then I say, "Sport demands lots of energy and I'm concerned you're not eating enough. You're too thin and need to fuel your body. Is there anything on your mind, darling?"

"No, Mum, I'm fine."

"I just want you to know, when I was your age, I stopped eating and became really obsessed with exercise. It made me sick, and I don't want that for you. At the time, my parents were divorcing and deep down I was hurting and trying to find some distraction from feeling so sad."

"Mum, I'm fine. I'm not you. I'm fine."

Anyone who is not fine will say they are fine! This is what scared humans do. Pretend all is well, soldier on and don't deal. It's how we survive as a species. It's a brilliant coping strategy, until it's not.

As soon as we get home, I pick up the phone and start to call for help. I'm hoping God will answer and tell me I'm overreacting and everything will be fine.

I call my husband. Then the school counsellor. Then a paediatrician friend. Then my mum. Afterwards, I drop the phone on the bed and start to cry. I'm tired of talking, explaining, convincing, problem solving, shame spiralling, and finally, blaming myself.

Our children are our mirrors. I'm terrified at what the mirror is reflecting back at me. What have I done? What am I still doing?

I need to nip it in the bud. Raise a red flag. Demand a time out. I can see all the cracks in the mirror and know that I put them there. I can't collapse on myself now and suffer for her. That weakens my fortitude and resolve. I am much better off focusing my energy towards seeking out opportunities for us to laugh, connect and nurture our spirits. I know I would put my life on the line to protect this child from the pain and suffering I have endured. Instead, I need to teach her how to feel the pain. I won't deny her this transformation. This healing is hers to claim. Perhaps the best thing to do right now is to hold all of it in the arms of compassion. We're going to love ourselves through this process and the right people will appear at the right time to help.

I recall a quote that James Baldwin says, *"Children have never been good at listening to their elders, but they never fail to imitate them."*

I wake up at a holiday house on the coast and I'm surrounded by the elements of earth and ocean, all the natural beauty that nurtures my spirit. Sitting around the fire one evening with my family and Mum, who is visiting, we watch the sun set while sharing a bottle of wine. I have been present to this welcome break from routine but still disturbed. My thoughts often swirl back to stories of self-blame and grasp for some sort of control as I watch my now teenager repeat so many of my own habits.

My mum comes to sit beside me at the fire and our conversation turns to this topic.

"I'm scared, Mum. I don't want Leila to suffer down the same path as I did. What did you do when I was experiencing this?"

Mum takes a sip of her wine.

"It was the toughest time in my life. I stopped everything. Healing you became the only focus. But you got through it, Tina. *You got* through it."

"How? I can't remember much because I think I blocked it out."

I sigh as tears prick the back of my eyes.

"Well, you were smart. You knew and listened and learned and realised you could. You were, and are, a smart person," Mum responded confidently.

I don't expect to hear the words 'you were smart', but it makes sense. I knew how to trust intelligence. Sure, I listened to the experts, the paediatrician and the psychologist, but ultimately, it was my own wisdom that turned around the disease.

As a child, my intuition was guiding me to make choices beyond my frightened thoughts. I decide that as well as attempting to feed Leila three serves of full fat dairy per day, as recommended by the dietician, I will feed her with charming intelligence. I'll show her how to access her own charm and know the difference between the voice that heals and the voice that harms.

I'll fill myself up with my own charm, so it overflows into her field. I'll choose charm over harm.

When parenting, you fall in love with a little person who is always changing and going through their own challenges. If your goal is to become more spiritful and chase the charm, which involves becoming more authentically you, then parenting offers that chance every day. Just when you've mastered play dates and sporting games, you need to learn about social media, Snapchat and online trolls. The rite of passage between your daughter's morphing from girl to teenager has no manual. You take it difficult decision by difficult decision, and you rely on your intuition.

I see this generation juggling new world complexities of cyber wars, climate catastrophes, vaping vampires, blown up lips, constant selfies, and the pressure to perform. It's why I want to wrap Leila in a cocoon and press pause on any further development. However, she's eating normally now, embracing all of life, throwing herself into every sport, absorbing friendships and giving so much of her spirit. That's my girl. Except I know she doesn't belong to me, and I can't claim her as 'mine'. She's her own little woman.

Leila came into the world fighting for her survival, with a scalped skull and a giant haematoma for a head. I wanted to breathe for her little lungs and swallow her sweet pain for her. I didn't want to accept we were two separate bodies and both helpless and dependent on a broken system to save us. Despite the traumatic birth, there's been a thirst for survival, growth and stubbornness since the day this fiery Aries baby arrived Earthside. From a tiny clingy human who wouldn't let me out of her sight, she's grown into a teenager who is now running away, out of my sight. It's confronting and an education at the same time. Each child is a little Buddha holding up a full-length mirror during every stage of their metamorphosis. You get to see exactly where you fall short and where your flaws are. Even when you're exhausted and confused, or peri-menopausal and full of self-doubt.

Am I a helicopter parent?
Am I too unconventional and disinterested?
Am I self-absorbed?
Am I teaching her how to be a control freak?
Am I on my phone too much?

Whatever needs to be transformed in your psyche and wherever you lack self-esteem will be revealed to you as a parent. When I began writing this book, I started to ask myself the questions above and slid into overwhelm. I knew I needed help with this conscious parenting thing, so reached out to Elena Brower, a beautiful being and phenomenal teacher. Our first session centred around acceptance, and it led to some interesting insights.

"Acceptance. Acceptance. Acceptance," Elena alerted, as she smiled and whirled her hand around the top of her head like a flashing siren. I started to laugh because once you see something, it becomes so obvious and you can't unsee it.

While I was busy nagging and trying to control what Leila ate, how she dressed and how much make-up she should wear, the tension and separation between us grew thick. I was practising the opposite of acceptance because I was afraid. Acceptance means we can be at peace with what is going right in our lives, and what is going wrong in our lives. The fear of practising acceptance stems from being passive in the face of difficulty, that if we're not worried or fearful, we won't be motivated to respond. However, a conscious parent can see their child causing harm to themselves, and instead of being driven by outrage, they can offer the child love and compassion. Even though I cannot control how much food my child leaves on her plate, I shifted my response.

I accept your choices.
You get to decide what you put in your body.
Whatever you choose, you have my full support.
I accept you exactly as you are, and I'm here for you.

The cracked mirror suddenly became clear. When I began using this language, I realised I had not been accepting myself. Unconsciously, I was projecting my own self-judgement and criticism onto my children, believing there was something 'wrong' or 'broken' and it was my responsibility to fix it. Deep down, believing that I too needed to be fixed. The reality is nothing is broken. Grandmothers and elders are the best teachers of this principle. Embodying a grandmother's heart represents overwhelming kindness, compassion, empathy and acceptance.

It was only after a weeklong stint with my Nan at her house that I began to heal from anorexia. The alchemy of turning around the trajectory of a chronic illness was found in the mystical realm of unconditional love. Nan didn't force me to eat breakfast, but I found myself picking up a piece of vegemite on toast and having a nibble. It tasted so good on white bread with butter that I asked for a second piece and saw Nan smiling to herself.

My mum came back to pick me up, and for the first time in a long while, saw me with shining eyes. My grandmother was the accepting balm I needed to turn around the aggression of the disease. Love healed, fear did not. What still makes an impact on me is remembering the wisdom on the back of a toilet door. Yep, on the back of the loo door at my Nan's hung a particular piece of writing which struck a chord. It was the *"Desiderata"*. As I sat on the loo doing 'God's business', I would look at the words and read the whole thing from start to finish with every visit.

The opening line made me feel calm.

Go placidly amid the noise and haste,
and remember what peace there may be in silence.

I gave myself the goal of learning it off by heart.

Speak your truth quietly and clearly,
and listen to others.

The most comforting line of all being ...

You are a child of the Universe no less than the trees and the stars; you have a right to be here ... it is still a beautiful world. Strive to be happy.

One of the main reasons I was drawn to studying with Dr Ricci-Jane Adams at the Institute for Intuitive Intelligence was the emphasis placed on self-esteem as the core function of intuition.

INTUITION + SELF-ESTEEM = INTUITIVE INTELLIGENCE

Self-esteem is not something we are born with. It is a lifelong journey which begins in childhood and has a learning process of empowering ourselves along the way. These levels or layers of power in us represent our empowerment journey. We begin with external self-esteem, internal self-esteem, collective self-esteem and Universal self-esteem. It takes strong-as-steel self-esteem to perceive differently than others and believe in the worth of our charming creature.

As a qualified Intuitive Guide, I've incorporated *Shadow Archetype Work* with hundreds of clients and found it to be very powerful at changing our relationship to fear. When we don't trust ourselves and our intuition, it is because we're hijacked by the fearful survival voices of our shadows. Fear blocks intuition. As you grow to confront and accept your own fears, you develop the intelligence to help others bring their fears out into the open, deal with them, and begin to dismantle them one by one. We often hear about the inner child, and when I immersed fully into my studies and spiritual work, I became aware that I don't just have an inner child—I have a team of them. Deep down, a part of us doesn't want to grow up and is driven to blame others for the reason our life is not 'working'.

Caroline Myss calls this 'woundology'. It holds us back from the emotional maturity we need to live our intuition. I know I didn't want to pass this down to my children, so did some further digging inside and made the discovery that my childhood was still very much active, and possibly interfering too much with my adulthood.

All our core beliefs are formed in childhood, and the more I explored, the more the inner child revealed itself, showing up in three dominant ways.

1. The Adult Child
This child takes on responsibilities to control and manage the future

because it doesn't see anyone else taking on that role, or doesn't trust grown-ups to protect them. The main feelings it creates are anxiety and panic.

2. The Wounded Child
This child is often abused, bullied, or sick and feels sorry for itself in order to stay dependent. It has an investment to keep the dead alive and stay in the past. The main feelings it creates are worthlessness and shame.

3. The Attached Child
This child hides its true feelings, bottles up, and people-pleases, so it's not rejected or abandoned. It constantly worries about what everyone else thinks and protects other people from its own negative emotions. The main feelings it creates are depression and sadness.

You can only take people as far as you've taken yourself, so I found some courage and dug deeper into my subconscious to meet my team of inner children. They became more specific and defined in their roles, and I started to see how they were keeping me in fear and competing with my voice of intuition and wisdom.

Adult Child: The Controlling Clipboard Child
The opposite of control is trust. When I'm not trusting my intuition, I'm gripping onto control and white-knuckling my way through anxious decisions. This child doesn't trust my inner adult, so feels the need to force everything into rigid and programmed schedules. This child also can't trust any other human being to do their job or show up in support, so she tries to do it all on her own. She recruits the addict as a way to sabotage any discomfort that uncertainty causes. After all,

numbing is the best form of control. If you don't feel the pain, there can't be anything wrong.

Right before I put myself in a leadership role, for example, prior to hosting a retreat, she often whispers, *'What are you doing? Why don't you just go on holidays? Let's open the bottle of wine.'*

Written on the clipboard are bullet point instructions to be checked off each day to ensure my sanity and mental health:

- Control
- Compare
- Criticise
- Compete

I will surely be graded on these criteria as part of my life assignment. Sticking to the protocol is paramount to staying out of the present time. I will only succeed if I worry relentlessly about the future.

Wounded Child: The Invisible Wounded Child

Staying wounded is like choosing to stay inside a cage even though the door is wide open. This child believes she is better off when she's hidden away from the big, bad world. She is a victim of everything that keeps happening to her. She strongly believes that nobody likes her, she'll be rejected, and she needs to work to suffocate the secrets that shame thrives on. If people knew the real her, they would run away. She doesn't even know the real her. She can't express what her needs are because her needs are even hidden from herself! So invisible, but so safe.

That girl is a ghost with unfinished business, lost in time and wandering between the rooms in my soul. She's knocking on all the doors in a giant warehouse of memories as if she needs to warn me of the future worries which will never happen.

Have you ever used an old wound or trauma to stay in your wounded child archetype? What benefit does this give you? The wounded stories are so ingrained it takes commitment and a stern, loving voice to get a response from this child.

Our charming creature would ask:
- How does staying in an old story enable you, dear one?
- What does blaming and punishing yourself give you permission to do?
- What are you gaining from empowering your wounds?

The answer eventually surfaces:
- If I believe I'm never good enough or that there's something wrong with me, I never need to take full responsibility for my life or grow up fully.

Attached Child: The Repressed Angry Child
Enter the peacekeeper. Somewhere along the line, this child picked up the belief that if she's a good girl and nice and polite, she'll be accepted and loved. This child senses tension before she even enters the room. She's an expert at putting on a smile and calming herself down, even though her boundaries have been violated, or someone is making her uncomfortable, or she doesn't agree with the opinions being shared. This child has pushed down so many feelings that she's actively building an inner volcano. It will be the final straw that breaks the camel's back, and she'll explode in violent eruptions, harming and maybe even punching people in her way. It's not pretty, and this is exactly the point. She's tried to stay pretty for too long. Pretty is poison.

It takes an enormous amount of energy when the inner kids run the show. They can quickly drain your spirit if you don't wake up to their agenda. Which is? To keep you 'safe'. Reparenting and tending to these inner children creates the safety they need to not be afraid. In the next chapter, I include dialogue and a guided meditation on how to do this.

These kids need to trust that you can stand up for them, protect them, manage conflict, enforce boundaries and speak the truth. Until your intuitive adult learns these powers, you'll continue to feel triggered and unconsciously shadow dance your way through relationships and self-doubt. Once they realise the esteemed adult in the room is capable of acting on their intuition, they all relax and stand down. Intuition can't function without this level of self-esteem because you need to be able to have the agency to trust your own choices.

PRACTICE

I am grateful for the one person who champions my creativity and growth: my mother. She found this poem in a box of childhood drawings and school archives:

"One day someone sat on me
She thought I was a rock
But I was not a rock
I was a turtle."

My grade one teacher comments, "I bet that hurt!"

This is evidence I already had an affinity with words from the get-go. While I relate more and more to my younger self, this short story is revealing. I was wired to feel and write about hurt and pain and charming creatures. If you asked me to paint a canvas of my inner children in their natural happy state, it would be on a beach. I imagine them barefoot in the sand at sunrise with wild bed-hair and wearing soft pastel pyjamas. They are standing in the sand dunes in the middle of a field of green sea grass. The fine strands dance in the gentle breeze around their little ankles. Their faces turn towards the morning sunlight, glowing with joyful peace on their rosy cheeks.

The following practice is designed to meet your shadow inner children and transform their overprotective fearful state back into creative charm.

CONNECTING WITH YOUR CHARMING CHILDREN

Which Shadow Child are you?

The Shadow Children

This is a guided meditation called, *'Which shadow child are you?'*

When we do this shadow work, we are going on a journey into the subconscious mind. As we know, this is where we tend to store all our core beliefs, stories and thoughts, which can be unhelpful when we are in fear, or our nervous system is dysregulated. So, we've identified three of these charming children that we all have, for they exist in everyone. They are the Attached Child, the Adult Child and the Wounded Child.

The Attached Child looks like the people pleaser. It's that part of us that represses emotion, often hard emotions, such as anger, and generally wants to keep everyone else happy and protected.

The Adult Child is that part of us that likes to control and worry about the future and grip and strive and really aim for perfection, which can set these unrealistic standards and create uncomfortable feelings.

The Wounded Child is that part of us that wants to retreat and be invisible, that can sit in self-pity, and that often just wants to hide from the world. We have all three of these charming children inside of us. And from day to day or week to week, we can have a different dominant one that can negatively control our lives in unhelpful ways.

> This practice helps you work with your shadow child and helps you to identify what it needs, so you can move on and repair yourself in a way that is nourishing, and that also leads you back to your highest intuitive self, which is powerful.
>
> 1. *Begin by taking a seat, a comfortable seat with back support, if possible. You can lie down for this as long as you stay conscious and aware of my voice. And as you settle in, closing*

down your eyes, take in a nice, deep breath, in through the nose and out through the mouth. Let your shoulders drop. Allow your neck to relax. Unclench your jaw. Soften your hands. Be aware of your whole body as a safe place to land in. Start to tune deep into your breath now, as you draw it into your belly on the inhale, and empty on the exhale, slowing it down, slowing it right down.

2. Bring your awareness now to your mind's eye. Just behind your eyes, notice that you are walking along a pathway, step by step, in a slow, meditative way. You are barefoot, following a path, only able to see one step in front of you. And as you walk along, you see a doorway ahead of you. Approaching the door, notice the colour, the size, the shape of the door. As you reach your hand out to touch the door, you open it. Curious, knowing that this is a portal or an opportunity to see more. What is it that you cannot see? As you step through the doorway, you find yourself at the top of a flight of stairs. You notice that this flight of stairs is on the coastline, your favourite beach in nature. You can see that these wooden stairs lead all the way down to the water at a beach. You know you're safe to explore this. It's almost as if you've been here before, smelling the sea salt, a soft breeze on your skin. You start to take one step at a time down the stairs, down, down, down, down, feeling the sand on the soles of your feet. You trust this path.

3. As you finally reach the bottom of the stairs, you stand in this soft, warm sand, letting it cover the tops of your feet. You continue to walk along the sand, down towards the water, hearing the waves crash even louder. Walking along this beach, up ahead, you start to see the outline of a person and a shape on the sand. As you walk closer, you are not afraid. And as you move even closer, you can see what looks like a big

sandcastle has been shaped and built. You walk all the way up to this sandcastle, which is just a few metres from the water. It's like a beautiful, big castle fortress. You notice that behind this sandcastle is a child, a child who has been busy building this sandcastle. You walk up to this child and find them covered in sand from head to toe. Their hair is matted with wet sand. There is sand all over their skin. This child looks up at you with caution. And naturally, you smile at the child, and you ask them, "How old are you?" Wait for that answer to appear.

4. *You kneel down so you are eye-level with this child who is standing about a metre away from you. You relax your arms. You ask the child, "Which of my shadow children are you?"*
"Are you the attached child, the adult child, or the wounded child?"
Wait for the answer to reveal itself.
You then ask the child, "When did you first show up in my life?"

5. *By this stage, the child is walking all the way up to hold your hand, and it's beginning to look more comfortable and relaxed as you continue to talk to it.*
You ask the child, "How are you feeling?"
"What emotions are you feeling?"

6. *Observe the child expressing in whatever way it wants to, whether that's through its voice or movement. By this stage, the water is washing up. As the sandcastle starts to dissolve, the waves wash away the fortress, the wall that this child has built. At the same time, the water washes the sand away from the child's body. The child is starting to look very clean. Now, free of all of that wet sand, the sandcastle is completely dissolved, washed out to sea. The child looks fresh and clean, eyes sparkling, hair all wet and neat and free of sand.*

7. You say to the child, "While you stay here and play, I'm just going to sit up in those sand dunes behind you, and you can come and join me whenever you're ready." You walk up the sand, finding a beautiful patch of sea grass on top of a sand dune. Making yourself comfortable, you stare out at the horizon as the child splashes around in the water and plays, looking full of energy and life. The child sits down with you, cross-legged, and smiles, eagerly waiting for a gift. You reach into your bag, pulling out a container of really cold watermelon. You both sit there and eat the watermelon on the beach together, spitting the pips out on the sand.

8. Finally, you ask the child, "What do I need to know for you to be free?" "What do I need to know for you to feel free?"

The child hops up and comes over to give you a hug. You wrap your arms around each other. This integration and melting begin to occur as both your bodies become one. And you can sit there, glowing in the sun, face tilted towards the sky, knowing it is safe for your shadow child to sit in the sand dunes, trusting that your wise current self is more than capable of making the wise choices.
The voice of unconditional love now says you are free.
Placing both hands over your heart, take in a nice, deep breath, in through the nose and out the mouth with a sigh, letting it all go. Through this journey, together, we return the shadow child back to the charming creature that is you.
I'm not afraid of the world outside.
Thank you ... Thank you ... Thank you ...

CHAPTER 2

CHARMING CHILDREN

> "Listen, are you breathing just a little and calling it a life?"
> —Mary Oliver

I walk into my younger daughter's room. She is lying on her bed with her laptop illuminating her wide, stunned eyes. It's 9.30 pm, past bedtime.

"What are you doing?" I ask.

"I have to finish homework. It's so bad I need to start again. I'm writing a story for English, and it needs to be nine-hundred words. I hate it. It's so bad."

Tears well up and spill over her cheeks. What could be so serious in year seven to cause this level of stress and angst? Then I remember what her teacher told me last week during the parent interviews.

"I've noticed signs of perfectionist tendencies around completing tasks and focusing on the numbers and the end result, instead of the process of learning. It seems to be more common in girls than boys. Often it appears during the transition to high school. All the expectations."

I sit on the bed beside Zoë.

"I know how frustrating it can be when the words don't flow and you don't know what to write. It's ok to take a break and not put this pressure on yourself. We often wake up so much fresher and inspired after a good night's sleep. You are much smarter than you think."

I am totally winging this parenting thing and can't help but worry now that she's trapped in her mind with unhelpful stories of 'not enoughness'.

Every word I tell her comes from the mother's heart of just wanting their child to be happy. I know I can't protect her from pain, but I can demonstrate how to talk to it.

Am I talking to myself in the same way?

I'm my child's biggest fan, but am I receiving advice from my inner fan in the same unconditionally loving way?

The opposite of self-esteem is powerlessness. One of the ways we protect ourselves as children is by proving that we're good enough. So often we become workaholics or perfectionist students or martyrs.

All the doing and saying, 'see me, see me' and proving our worth is a way of not feeling and avoiding our real need to offer ourselves this attention. Protecting ourselves from not feeling hard emotions turns into external control. However, we never really have control. All we have is a child clinging to a clipboard.

Author Elizabeth Gilbert has a practice she shares called 'letters from love'. It's how you can give the voice of unconditional love a way to communicate with your inner children. As I made this part of my daily spiritful practice, I found that addressing each individual part was very helpful. If we don't tend to these younger parts of us, they end up haunting us.

Over time, I adapted 'letters from love' to be 'letters from charm'.

If charm had a voice, what would she say to her children?
To answer this question, it's like another Self needs to be invited into the inner family experience.

Who is your Charmed Self?

Visualise her.

For me, I can almost picture her standing in front of me. She is someone who is always in the background, waiting in the wings. She's full of grounded peace and calm confidence. Her presence is a refuge of safety. She's ready for a real conversation. I turn to her for guidance, but she is mostly silent. Her body language holds enough magic and power that she's 'enough' just for existing. She witnesses all the fear in these overprotective inner children with fierce compassion. A Self whose kind, steady gaze penetrates the very centre of my being and refuses to look away from pain. A charming embodiment so knowing and embracing of all my shadowy parts.

Every day she looks at these three children and asks ... *How do you feel? What do you need today?*

Holding them all with connection and unconditional love, she becomes the parent to my inner children like we do to our own kids or pets.

If charm had a voice, she would say to them:
- *You are loved. You are safe.*
- *You are free to play and relax.*
- *You are safe, even when other people are disappointed with your decisions.*
- *You are still loved, even when others reject you.*
- *You are a child of love, my sweet little sea grasses.*
- *There's no need to worry or stay wounded.*
- *I'm just going to keep talking to you because I know how quickly you forget that you don't need to protect me.*

These protective parts are comforted by loving words, but they also need to feel useful. They are so used to working overtime for you that they relax quicker if you also give them another purpose.

Here are some examples I use to commune with my charming children

Controlling Clipboard Child – to the part of me that feels anxious and fearful.

I can't imagine the fear and uncertainty you have had to face in your life, but you got through it. I'm sorry you had to go through that experience. It's so understandable that you are trying to protect me. I acknowledge the strength of you. You don't need to be scared anymore. It's ok, I'm here now. I'm awake to you. I will protect you and keep you safe. I invite you to slow down your breathing, relax your hands and stop managing. There is nothing to control. You can count on me to be capable. There is no need to be unsafe anymore. I set you free.

I know you love a job to do, so I'm going to suggest something different. That pen and clipboard you clutch in your hands can be used to create magic. Allow your hand to be moved by a different energy that has nothing to do with fear. Relax the grip of your fingers and notice how your pen becomes a conduit for your charming creature to dance with. Change the clipboard from a shielded weapon to a creative tool. You can draw me a picture. You can sketch your favourite place in nature and make beautiful art. You can write me a story. This is your work, my child. You are an incredible artist. That clipboard is your easel. The pen, a magic wand.

Repressed Rage Child – to the part of me that is angry and rageful.

I see you. Thank you for being brave and courageous enough to handle this level of emotion. I can only imagine what you have been through in the past that has caused you to feel this way. I want you to put down this internal fight now. You are valid to have felt this anger and we can put down the armour now. There is nothing to brace against. It is safe for you to express this fire inside you and we can move forwards now. That was the past. Thank you for protecting me. I've learned the lesson. It is safe for you to communicate boundaries and honour your feelings. I choose to set you free. I set you free.

I know you love a job to do, so I'm going to suggest something different. The opposite of repression is expression. You have suppressed your voice for too long and it has caused an ache in your jaw. Open your mouth wide now and sing. This is your holy task, to create harmony and music with your emotions. You have a powerful instrument. Now let it be heard. What song does your soul make? It can be both loud and powerful or soft and simple. I know you think nursery rhymes are uncool, so let the rage turn into rap, rock 'n' roll or R 'n' B. Express your fire and let the flames belt out of your belly as you hold your hairbrush and scream into the mic. This is your show, my darling, and you are the star.

Invisible Wounded Child – to the part of me that has felt victimised and shameful.

I can't imagine what made you feel so powerless and the traumas you have endured. I see how they have resulted in shrinking yourself and staying hidden and small. No more. I love you and support you to release this shame. You did the best you could with the resources you had in the moment. It's not your fault. I forgive you and invite you to be who you are. It's safe to be you. You are loved always. You are enough. You are free.

I know you love a job to do, so I'm going to suggest something different. All that shame and blame you've internalised wants to find its way out. Your work is to open your arms wide now and hug everyone hello. Hugging and touching safe people will let the love out that has been locked up and unseen. Hug to be visible and take up space. Open your arms wide and turn your wounds into wise, compassionate action. Hug your fellow sisters and brothers and be the embrace of grace. Notice how your power returns to you when you give love to others. Now do the same for yourself. You must include *you* in your hugs, even if this has never been modelled to you. Use your hands to rub the skin on your arms. It feels nice, doesn't it? Your arms and hands are like a love language extending directly out from your heart line. This is how wounds are aired and healed into scars. Hugging over hiding is your medicine and magic role. I love you.

When we think of spirit—the Universal intelligent energy, the light source, the shakti—as an abstract force, it may seem impressive but not very approachable. We experience ourselves as this energy of 'oneness' in fleeting moments when we're in flow, on the yoga mat or having a really good day, but then it quickly slips through our fingers. How do we think bigger than our own limited bodies, insecurities and personas? Science keeps telling us that we're made of star dust, but my rational brain is challenged by this fact.

Now think of that same energy as your charming creature and the whole situation moves from impersonal to intimately personal. It becomes more playful, childlike and less serious. You're not as intimidated to get to know it, invite it to brunch, introduce it to others and have an ongoing relationship with it.

Just imagine for a moment that you have not seen your creature for a long time. You've forgotten exactly what she feels like. She has gone astray, or worse, she's been caged up somewhere, captured by another owner or identity.

You have lost the spark in your eyes, the bounce in your step, the enthusiasm that gets you up in the morning. Life feels repetitive, dull, flat and boring. You start to look for the charm outside of yourself.

You try eating more food, drinking more wine, scrolling through social media, shopping online, anything for a charming dopamine hit. You become desperate for someone else to give you their charm. Hoping for their approval and attention. Hoping to be told what to do rather than listening to your own guidance. Searching for the charm becomes a crime-solving mission.

Who's taken it? It must be someone else's fault. I'll blame my mother, my teacher, my dog because it is always demanding to be fed. All of a sudden, I'm a victim looking to be 'uncharmed'. I start to find evidence of this everywhere. There must be a reason why my life is so uncharming. It doesn't occur to me yet that as an owner of a charming creature, I am responsible for taking care of it.

What the charming creature craves is creative expression and freedom. When we are constantly in survival mode, creativity is starved and locked up. This force needs to be given movement and flow, not stagnation. Staying authentic to where the energy wants to lead us will nourish our intuition. Choosing the charm will fuel our spirit.

What fuels our spirit?

Truly being who we are and not doing what is expected of us.

Too many women don't take their charm seriously and instead become society's shock absorbers and stress containers. Charm turns into a poison if it doesn't flow out of you. If you don't find a way to express it, it will cause disease and kill you. How fluent we are with this language is the secret to flourishing and being Spiritful. The charm excites and propels us forwards.

If I asked you to bring me your charm in a backpack, what would you put in it?

It's physically impossible because it exists in a much more subtle dimension which is why we need to have faith in its unique love language.

When we return to our charm, we discover something we can trust, something so unique and delightful that no one can take it away. And from this charm comes the clarity to remember and the courage to offer your true expression to the world.

As children, we're taught that being charming is reserved for princes and princesses. We were fed a fantasy. Fables full of fictional characters wanted to make us believe it was unobtainable. Nothing could be further from the truth. You don't need to be told by culture that you have earned the charm. Every being is born into it because every soul is sovereign and capable of rescuing itself through remembrance of its origin, Universal source or bliss. Anytime you follow your bliss, charm is there. Be seduced by this essence. Let the charm fill up your cup.

"What we need right now is more women who have detoxed themselves so completely from the world's expectations that they are full of nothing but themselves. What we need are women who are full of themselves. A woman who is full of herself knows and trusts herself enough to say and do what must be done. She lets the rest burn."

—Glennon Doyle

The work of intuition requires you to accept your flaws, but it also demands you accept your fullness. Within this fullness is your charming creature. We'll only keep up with the speed of change that is sweeping the world if we chase the charm. Charm may be just the antidote to a negative spiral of survival, judgement and criticism.

Charm is how we live our intuition because it's honest. The reason we're attracted to 'charming' is because somewhere deep inside, the truth seduces us. We long to not be afraid of the outside world but to spread love and connect with the things that lift us up.

Later in this book, you'll learn the seven ways to live your intuition and be your charming creature. In a society predicated on the personal pursuit of seeking spirituality, as if it were a fugitive on the run, it can be hard to discern what the charming creature actually feels like, how it already lives and breathes in us. Our society is based on dangling this carrot in front of us and convincing us that our charm is in the next thing we buy or person we believe. Chasing the charm suggests it is unobtainable, and it's not. It's right there inside us.

When I'm quiet and still, I can hear charm's voice chime in.
> *Hey you little charm chaser, stop chasing me. Let me chase you for once. Let my charming chariot pick you up when you least expect it. Put down your desperate driven strategies. I know you have an insatiable hunger to strive for spirit and seek it in quirky far away corners. But notice that the name is spiritual seeker, not spiritual finder. The path is the goal and your energy, well your spiritful energy, doesn't lie, does it? Charm is an inner change agent. It's going to point you back to the truth and away from the next shiny dazzling object. It's going to say 'stay right where you are and don't move.' Remember what you told your daughters when they were five and six in the shopping centre? If you get lost, or confused or can't see me, stay right where you are against a wall, I'll come get you. This, my darling charming child, is how all reunions take place and safety is restored. I'm coming for you. Sit. Be silent. Put your back against the wall. And breathe. Love, your charming creature.*

How does the charm make itself known to you?

Some of you may be wondering if this creature is the same thing as an animal. The answer is no, but animals do have a purpose and a role to play. An animal is a spirit creature you have an encounter with or experience a divine connection with because they embody an esoteric quality that you're attracted to. Or they simply love you unconditionally. Spirit creatures have something to teach us. Spirit creatures don't look to social media or the scales to know their value. Their value rests in existence by simply being creatures. Animals reflect back to us a part of our charming creature we want to nurture and grow into. Animals empower and inspire our own inner charm so we can express it outwardly more freely. We often borrow power from animals until we can cultivate it ourselves.

Children are the perfect example of this practice. My youngest daughter was five years old when she became obsessed with horses—not uncommon for a girl that age. Every birthday was gifted with horse-riding lessons, and posters adorned her walls of thoroughbreds in every colour and stance. Predictably, she begged for the equestrian lifestyle that our inner-city dwelling and budget were incapable of providing.

One weekend, I watched her cantering down the hallway of our house enthusiastically. She shook her head, causing her long blonde hair to shake and fly behind her as she made a fluttering sound through her lips.

"C'mon, Styler," she said to herself. "Let's go join the others at the top of that hill. There'll be some greener grass up top for lunch."

Except she wasn't talking to herself. Styler was her imaginary friend, an invisible horse which never left her side for the next four or five years. Styler slept next to her bed on a grey round rug, ate breakfast with the family every morning and spontaneously appeared out of the boot of the car during day trips to the beach.

This imaginary friend played an important role for my daughter. It fed her charming creature with confidence and trust in her own animal instincts. Every time Styler was present, she was living her intuition. When she turned ten, Styler began to fade away and we heard less and less of the galloping human hooves down the hallway. Through no fault of our own, as we get older, we become conditioned and massaged into the noisy world around us. We become obsessed with what other people think of us. This is insane because we can't control other people's opinions or judgements, so why would we lose energy focusing on it?

Worrying about how others perceive you is the same as telling yourself ... *I'm going to base my success and happiness on whether or not some stranger is having a good or a bad day.* That is a high-risk choice for your one wild and precious creature.

When you carry on along this trajectory, after a while, something inevitably happens. Sometimes it's a whisper from Spirit. Perhaps a little niggle that it's time to look within, or a big spiritual kick up the backside to show you that how you're living your life just doesn't fit anymore. Like a pair of old shoes that are too tight, you don't recognise your own personal package has altered to become more digestible to those around you. You have disconnected from the charm. It takes self-esteem to transcend these worries. Especially when it's the people we care about the most, such as family or close friends, who question our decisions, our lifestyle choices, or the changes we've adopted since growing out of old habits. Intuition is not interested in watching you enact some personality performance in order to conform with an imagined idea about how a charming person looks or behaves. Becoming spiritful is about becoming self-authorising. It's about becoming *you*.

Being spiritful means being fuelled by this inspiration even when you are not prepared for its arrival. The word inspiration comes from the Latin *inspirare* which translates to breathe in or blow into. This whisper might catch you as a brief moment of inspiration that sneaks through the back door of your soul when you aren't looking.

It was this whisper from spirit that led me to dive into the powerful practice of breathwork. I craved a new experience of altered consciousness that could transcend me from malaise and my own mental prison of ego thinking.

We inhale creative energy with every breath and as the air moves, so the old dreams stir and the inner flame fans. When this air is charged with blessing and longs to bless another, we know our spirit is trying to wake us up. It's a spiritful awakening. Spending more time filling our spirits, rather than trying to impress people, is within our control and much more nourishing for our charming creature. If we try to intellectualise this experience, it is like trying to strip the ocean of its waves. Spirit and charm have nothing to do with 'I' or 'me'.

"Most transcendent experiences are completely ego-free. In the moment, we lose track of time and space, we lose track of our bodies, we lose track of our selves. We dissolve. And yet … spirituality emerges from consciousness and the material brain. And the paramount signature of consciousness is a sense of self, an 'I-ness' distinct from the rest of the cosmos. Thus, curiously, a thing centred on self creates a thing absent of self."

—Alan Lightman

Human beings have a hunger for truth and transcendence. We long for connection to something beyond the self as the crucible of our transcendent experiences. Much of what happens to us in life is nameless because our vocabulary is limited, and we don't have a language for it. Most mystical experiences get told out loud, beginning with 'It was like …' because the storyteller hopes that the telling of the story in metaphor can transform a nameless event into a familiar or intimate one.

Regardless of what frightens our charming creatures during childhood, it is possible to experience transcendence. It is possible to experience Post Traumatic Growth (PTG) and mature from fear to freedom. Rather than shrinking in the face of life's challenges, it is a type of transcendence that transforms negative experiences into positive change. This exploration uncovers meaning and purpose as well as spiritful growth and a new appreciation for life. Rather than going through our challenges, we grow through them and find ourselves able to live authentically and follow our charm. But first, we must learn to reparent ourselves. We must go on a quest to find the inner intuitive adult. Reparenting, or perhaps even parenting ourselves for the first time, is what cultivates the safe environment to coax out the creature from its cave. Charm needs to feel safety to express itself, so developing relationships with these younger parts is explored throughout the chapters of this book.

Your charm can never be destroyed by somebody else. It only ever changes from one form to another. Just when we think we've got it all worked out, it will transform yet again, inviting us into the deeper mystery to 'know thyself'. Every couple of years, I feel this strong spiritual impulse to peel back another layer as evolution moves me to ask these unanswerable questions.

Who am I?

Why am I here?

The spiral continues as we find ourselves seeking our changing charm once more.

None of us are grown-ups, only ever growing up, and when I began writing this book, I questioned whether I was having a midlife spiritual crisis. My intuition has always raised red flags over the possibility of a midlife mountain. Isn't that what our culture expects when we reach our mid-forties? I dismissed it because surely, I'd already had my midlife mountain—a health burnout, drug addiction and career backflip in my late thirties. Done and dusted.

At the risk of renouncing my worldy possessions and becoming a hopeless seeker escaping the cliche of midlife crisis, I wondered whether I was on a similar path?

Travel. It is the constant invitation that niggles my soul. Certain lands often draw, magnetise and call us in to connect with, walk on and feel their cultures. But these lands wanted to draw something out of me as well.

The sensuality of embodied divine femininity: shakti, pleasure, and devotion. The qualities that, for a woman in her mid-forties, need raging attention. Love of life, the essence of it, was asserting itself all over me. I craved animated authenticity in the truest form. I craved for my charming creature to take reign. While I was totally preoccupied proving my existence in all the different roles of mother, teacher, wife, business owner, leader, mentor, sister, daughter, writer, healer, dog walker and terrible cook, my intuition was gently tapping me on the shoulder again and whispering ... "Um, you're pretending." I didn't suffer enough to be diagnosed with clinical depression, anxiety or even early menopause, but the distance between truth and reality was uncomfortable as hell.

Somehow, the Universe knew how to break open all this pretending with a teenage daughter who was mirroring my coping strategies as I dealt with one professional rejection after another, the rollercoaster of writer's block, and the chronic need to nap every day just to keep walking and act like everything's fine. There was a time in my life where all these events would have overwhelmed the shit out of me, and I would have hidden myself away or numbed out. It's been my intention for the last five years to notice the resistance when it surfaces, and to meet it with the love, nourishment and prayer I'm born to receive abundantly.

I must say, I am grateful to the past version of myself who set that intention.

If you're grappling with a midlife mountain and outgrowing old fears, I honour you. Don't forget to thank your younger selves, too. The path ahead demands an opening to choose your charming creature over pretending habitual ways of being.

The question is, how real are you prepared to be?

Will you travel into the depths of your charming creature with me?

PRACTICE MEDITATION

Charming Creature Meditation

This is a practice to experience your own power.

I want you to take your shoes off and connect into this power right now.

Close your eyes and take three conscious breaths, sensing the heartbeat of the earth through your soles.

Place both hands over your heart.

Your heart is the centre of your intuition.

Bring to your heart-mind something or someone that cultivates a feeling of gratitude or charm.

It could be a person or an event or a place in nature.

Allow this sensation to expand.
Connect into the subtle field of something beyond the boundary of your skin.

Now imagine, if charm had a face, what would it look like?
If you were to see yourself as a charming creature, how would you move?

What does the voice of your charming creature sound like?
How does your charming creature express its gifts and unique talents?
Can you lean into these sensations and feel as if you already are embodying this creature?

Is it safe?
Is it loving?
Is it kind?

Now ask your charming creature:
"What do you want me to know?"

Allow the answers to be revealed in sensation, rather than thought.
What is the next best choice for you to make?

Notice the emotions that are building within you. Observe the part of you that is witnessing this experience and repeat the words ... Thank you ... Thank you ... Thank you ...

Gently take a big breath in and a loud and looooong sigh out.

JOURNAL PROMPT

1. Can you imagine a life where you feel more relaxed, confident, less afraid, at ease and fully aligned with your values? What would expressing your natural charm feel like?

2. Describe a day in the life of your charming creature that reflects this existence. Don't hold back here. Really imagine how you'd wake up, where your environment is, who you interact with and what your conversations are like. Give yourself permission to dream big and imagine this reality like it's happening in your body.

3. Write about an animal that came into your life and taught you something about acceptance, love and death.

CHAPTER 3

21 DAYS IN THE DESERT

> "The two risks of travel are disappointment and transformation. The fear you'll be the same person when you go home, and the fear you won't."
> —Kate Harris

In 2022, I turned forty-three years old and decided to spend three weeks of that year walking in the Australian desert on the infamous Larapinta Trail. This impressive hike of about two hundred and thirty kilometres weaves its way through the MacDonnell Ranges. Located in the Northern Territory in central Australia, it's known as the heart of the nation and the heart of our culture. It's where the First Peoples—the Aboriginal and Torres Strait Islander communities—celebrate our millennia-old laws and customs. This land was never given to the colonisers by the Traditional Owners and is sacred. It is and always will be Aboriginal Land. I wanted to learn the protocols, to see, feel, touch, taste, embrace and unlearn all that had blocked my own heart from receiving this spirit.

It was vastly outside of my comfort, but my intuition was relentless in leading me to this land. I committed to this challenge. It was the risk I needed to take. It felt like the grown-up adult thing to do. Perhaps an overdue initiation was required to reckon with my past and fill a bigger pair of spiritful boots. These twenty-one days were made up of three separate 'Hero's Journeys' to Arrernte Country, where I hiked sections of one of the Great Walks of Australia. On two out of the three, I was leading retreats. The other one was with my best mate, continuing our Camino pilgrimage, but this time closer to home. Travelling back to Spain was not going to happen during this pandemic, which was a blessing for some Australians who got to appreciate their own backyard and culture for a change.

Walking is a form of knowing and a process of losing oneself. It's not a mistake to become lost on purpose but rather an active embrace of the landscape itself. Trading in the compass you hold in your hand for the one you make with your feet. In this way, as you follow your intuition rather than a plan, you're thrust into a position to discover what you didn't know you needed. You're thrown into challenges and discomfort as life asks you to discard your crutches. The difficulties of a pilgrimage are what ultimately make it so rewarding. In embracing courage, you find that nothing can compare to discovering your own inner strength and resilience.

The fumbling forwards on foot changes your relationship with yourself. That's how it humbles and inspires you. This humility need not be humiliating. Instead, it's a quiet process that leaves you more likely to confront fears and less likely to avoid them out of dull habit or complacency. It fuels transformation.

Inevitably, this leaves the pilgrim more open-hearted and less judgemental, more curious and less controlling, trusting of a power much greater than you.

The great poet Rumi asks, *"Would you become a pilgrim on the road to love? The first condition is that you make yourself humble as dust and ashes."*

In preparation for leading the first retreat, I pack and repack my red North Face bag several times, ensuring not one item is missing. Poles, socks, gaiters, an entire pharmacy, warm woollies, lightweight stuff and hiking boots. The whole kitchen-sink approach is not sitting well with me, so I reverse the process, throwing cargo overboard to lighten the Airbus and fuel my minimalist fantasies.

As the plane begins to descend over Arrernte Country, the nervous butterflies in my stomach flutter. This is the first camping retreat experience in a remote location I've ever led, and my sister, Peta, is sitting next to me. The rows in front and behind us are filled with our retreat group. The plane is alive with eager chatter and an excited energy coming through my seat.

Peta is three and a half years older than me. Always the 'big sister' by birthing order, she is not on this retreat. As leader of the group, I become her big little sister. I ask everyone on board to put down their roles. Nobody is big sister, mother, daughter, employee, or boss during this time. We take turns in being the one who supports and the one who needs support. We take turns in the one teaching little feet how to walk and the one teaching big hearts how to open. Becoming big little sisters to each other is a sort of soul contract that transcends age, numbers and hierarchy. This is how sisterhoods are formed and instant families are made.

Peta squeezes my hand and asks, "Are you excited to meet Dylan?"

Dylan is the host of the camp and owns the hiking organisation. We first spoke a year ago, when this vision prompted me to seek a First Nations guide to create this experience with.

For the last twelve months, we have only chatted on the phone with many calls, many stories and many discussions around how this collaboration will unfold. Me sharing with him the work I do and the power of retreats. Him sharing about his family, his business, the beauty of walking on his land, the history of Aboriginal people. There had been an eruption inside me and a real thirst to understand Indigenous knowledge and the oldest continuing culture on the planet.

I began having many dreams of being guided by an Aboriginal elder as I allowed my spirit to be consumed by learning what had been hidden in Australian history. I was craving to be liberated from the confusing timeline of both my modern self and our ancient place in this world.

"Yesss, I can't believe we are going to meet in person finally," I reply.

As the wheels of the plane touch down, our group disembarks in anticipation of the seven days ahead. This group of twenty is made up of nineteen women and one man, all clients and students I know and have worked with. Mothers and daughters, best friends, husband and wife, entrepreneurs, soul companions, sisters and business bosses. We sit in camp chairs around an open fire with full bellies after the first dinner, sipping tea as we settle into our new environment. The colours of the sunset are the most stunning blend of pink blush, violet, gold and yellow. It's almost pointless trying to capture it all on our phones as we discover it changes too quickly, as if deliberately dodging our attempts at documentation.

The enormous plains of planets move in the dark sky above us like stars of navigation. The rounding moon shines an illuminated glow upon the faces in the circle while the fire warms our toes. Dirt cakes itself onto our feet as the soil below is red and dusty. I can already feel a layer of it covering my clothes and hair as we breathe in the powdery earth greeting us.

The day had been long, up early at sunrise to travel and reach our destination in the remote central desert. With no access to the internet, our bodies are adjusting to a vibration of silence. Dylan approaches the circle and takes hold of a stick to draw a blueprint of his family's kinship system in the red dust. He points from the drawing to the ridged mountain ranges, illustrating where creation originated sixty thousand years ago. With less than ten words, an entire timeline of the remote past is filled in with this simple diagram. Seeing through our untrained eyes, on the ground at our feet is a map of human history and stories.

I look around the circle at this group of people and my heart stretches to accommodate our own collective stories. I momentarily forget my life back home, the stressors, the struggles and the schedule that now seems insignificant. The sound of quiet chatting and engaged conversation already carry us to a deep connection we are yet to discover will be our life raft.

We are linked in a circle of healing and group intention. On a deep cellular level, all are there for reasons beyond our mind. The spirit of the land is already ebbing and flowing in our words and in our breath. I imagine this is what community has always looked like. Ancient and simple. And driven by an innate hunger to discover our real, authentic, spiritful nature grounded in our primal existence. We begin to drift away from seeking the altered meditative states and trade the seduction of the transcendent for the earthly and ordinary. Leaving behind one way of living and preparing for another. We know we need to make our way to the desert to walk all day and sit all night until the landscape reveals itself, not as vast or empty but full of spirit and presence. The formidable terrain of the desert puts us in our place and reminds us how tiny we really are.

We've not geared ourselves towards any particular climax, reaching the top of a mountain or conquering all two hundred and thirty kilometres of trail. Rather, this Hero's Journey is about becoming more present with the ground. Accepting gravity in each step is a way to practise presence. This Hero's Journey is focused on not pushing through, but having the choice to leave the path, pause, and seek rest or respite if needed. It's A Hero's Journey about leading others through their own experience and allowing them to march in front, following their instincts and inner compass.

I imagine myself as a walking science experiment in real time. Moving to feel moved but also needing to find my blisters before my bliss. Placing myself in situations where I embrace challenge and can teach and learn from a place of the unknown and vulnerable exposure. We travel to leave our habits behind. Being creatures of habit is both a blessing and a curse. The habitual creature always seeks security, routine and certainty at the cost of the inner charming creature craving adventure and inspiration of the unknown. We travel enthusiastically to be transformed and free of our identities and personas. Confronting ourselves again for the first time is to be both lost on purpose and set adrift to course correct.

Everyone drawn to the heart of our country has come in search of their unique true north; we are bound together by what motivates us. It doesn't matter if we have different spiritual beliefs or opinions, we are all walking together in the same direction.

As the energy quietens and silence begins to surround us, a catching yawn signifies it is time to retire into our swags for the night and welcome a good night's sleep. Everyone is keen to be up early and prepare for the first day's hiking adventure. I stand up from my chair and follow the light from my headtorch towards my tent. Fumbling at the zippers to find the opening, I can hear a symphony of zip-zip sounds as we all cautiously ensure no tent flaps are left open. I don't know why the sound of the zippers causes me to hold my breath. The presence of snakes and creatures of the night waiting for any opportunity for a sheltered home is too real to risk leaving tent doors casually open.

Preparing for bed is a collective effort of teeth brushing under the stars, flashing torch headlights, bush wees and the rustling of backpacks as gear is carefully packed and prepared for the following morning. Spinifex appears as curated grass, but its needle-sharp leaves are waiting to pierce through any backside attempting to find a spot to squat. I gratefully slide into my swag, navigating more zippers and a lumpy pillow, but I can't wipe the smile from my face.

We're here finally. We're really doing it. As the camp site quietens down, I close my eyes but cannot sleep. I'm too excited. Thoughts of tomorrow whiz through my mind—wait—what the hell was that? Scurrying—*inside* my tent—near my foot. My heart races. I am not alone. My eyes bulge out of my skull trying to see in the dark. I reach my left hand out from under the doona covers and feel for my headtorch. More scurrying in the far corner of the tent.

"No! Please don't let there be a mouse trapped in here. I hate mice. This is shit. I'm not going to be able to get to sleep and I'll be tired on the first day of retreat. How am I supposed to be a good teacher when I can't even be calm and peaceful? Why is this happening to me?"

My thoughts go round and round.

I fiddle for the torch button and beam the bright light up to the ceiling and around the four tented walls. Only a flimsy piece of khaki nylon separates me from the mighty majestic wilderness. An illuminated beam searches for evidence of anything suspect. This creature knows now it is being hunted and silence prevails. As we play the game of cat and mouse, a wave of determination comes over me.

I realise I am trapped inside this camping shelter with my ego mouse. This is the same mouse Ganesha the elephant uses to ride as a vehicle and overcome fear obstacles. Ganesha is the Hindu elephant-headed God deity known as the remover of obstacles. In traditional mythology, the lowly rat is his mount who irritates him into enlightenment. My panicking mind has manifested into a furry rodent far from the grounded charming creature well equipped to lead a meditation class at sunrise. As the fearful thoughts ruminate and turn into stories of *'Why am I doing this in the middle of nowhere'* *'What were you thinking Tina?' 'You're going to fail'* and *'You're not strong enough for this'*, the veils of illusions are becoming heavier and angrier.

These voices get louder until I decide to stop them in their tracks.

How can I quieten the loud, scared inner voice and lovingly show it there is a much more expanded world outside?

Tina, be the hunter, not the hunted. I try to interrupt the mousey mind-chatter.

"C'mon, you little critter, you will not get away with this. Come out, come out, wherever you are ..."

Suddenly, a sliding sound down a nylon slippery dip suggests something is breathing straight in front of me. I shine the torch at the door and there, right in the middle of the centre zip line, is a frozen brown fieldmouse, clinging on vertically to the fabric with all four tiny hands.

"Ha!" I say out loud. "Found you!"

Now I need to figure out how to get it out.

After only a few more moments, I succeed with some strong swear words and a graceful swooshing swipe of my trunk as I slice open the front door to my tent.

"Fucking fly, little one."

Alone again.

Eventually, I surrender and fall asleep. The next morning, I wake to the shrill yipping of howling dingoes permeating the campsite. The sound gives me goosebumps and makes the hair on the back of my neck stand on end. Australia is said to be the only country where wild dogs take their place with such noise and ownership. Our native charming creatures can act with fierce love when it comes to protecting their territory. Given temperatures can reach the mid-forties in an arid summer, the variety of charming creatures that can survive out here is incredible. One by one, the sound of the zip-zip and another head pops out of a tent to take the first step into day one of their desert retreat. The usual habits of checking a phone, getting ready for work or wrangling children into uniforms are absent, and we eagerly anticipate the newness of each morning minute.

I hear voices chime in.

"Good morning! Wow, look at the colours in the sky!"

"Is the hot water boiled?"

"I can't find my yoga mat!"

"I never want to leave."

Preparation begins as boots, daypacks and water bladders are thrown around. I'm organising myself while conscious of the group's readiness to hike and whether two litres of water or three will be the difference between dehydration or an extra unnecessary weight on my back. I can feel sweat and moisture building already under my jacket, so I take it off to tie round my waist. It's only seven thirty, but the sun is beaming straight onto us with no clouds in sight. My feet are still tender from a previous hike, and I massage them before strapping into suffocating shoes for the day. A big, black toenail looks like it's finally ready to fall off after an ongoing infection caused by a poor choice of boots. I give it a little tug and it lifts off the nail bed completely revealing fresh baby skin underneath. Another little tug and it comes off in the grip of my fingers.

"Damn," I say out loud.

I put it back in its place like a missing jigsaw piece and wrap a Band-Aid around the throbbing toe while trying to remember where I packed the ibuprofen. While I secure my poles, the final snacks and first aid supplies in the bag, I pause for a moment and take in the organised chaos around me. We're all in this together as supplies are shared around, laces are tied, sunscreen applied, straps and gaiters, yoga mats and journals are all shoved into each other's backpacks. We are here to become lighter versions of ourselves, but obviously we need some essentials for the journey ahead.

A whistle sounds from the food truck.

"The walk today is cancelled," the camp director shouts at our group.

Everyone freezes and turns their heads in the same direction. There is silence and blank faces and a few darting eyes between myself and my leaders.

"It's getting too hot and you're taking too long to get ready. We can't hike in this heat at the rate we're going. You are all too relaxed!"

It is true that even for May, these unseasonal, high, searing thirty-degree temperatures are unexpected and make hiking in the desert potentially dangerous and unsafe.

We all pause to take in this information. From the looks on our faces, we can't help feeling shocked, frustrated and disappointed. I'm not sure whether being too relaxed on day one of this retreat is a compliment or a criticism, but it matters not.

Take a breath, Tina, I say to myself as a flappy, frantic bird is trapped inside my chest. There is no schedule. There is no schedule. There is no schedule. I am going with the flow.

Except, obviously, there *is* an agenda and time *is* of the essence when we're following the movements of the searing sun and the safest times to move beneath it. Contradictions and paradoxes are everywhere. I don't understand why things are happening the way they are. All I can do is trust we are in the right place at the right time. We discuss plan B and gather to look at our options for the day ahead. I can sense tension fuelled by different personalities and uncertainty.

One of my strengths as an intuitive and leader is that I can read a room like the back of my hand. Picking up on other's moods and emotions was a survival skill I learned as a child. I can tell how people feel before they even know it themselves. It is not a superpower, rather it's an energetic wiring I'm tuned into, which developed into the unwanted trait of being a people pleaser as an adult. It's a conditioning that took much unravelling but still comes in useful during these types of situations. Everyone needs to breathe, I realise. They are ripe for it. Some would even say 'triggered'.

"If we can't walk the Larapinta section, we'll do a breathwork class instead," I say.

There is some resistance to this idea with Dylan, and we continue to play this game of mental tennis back and forth, trying to get both our needs met. I apply my masterful skill at appealing to someone else's charming creature, coaxing it out of their armoured and protective cave to disarm its defence. I soften its exterior so that it turns to butter and melts back to trusting the hand that feeds it.

Some creatures hide away because they are scared. We know the charm is there because we've connected with it before, but fear will frighten it when it feels out of control. Control becomes a coping mechanism for creatures that have endured a lot of trauma in their life. When we see past the reactive and defensive creature, we can ask the question, "What is it that hurt you in the past?" It is the responsibility of the charm to recognise the spirit in all creatures and act with compassion and curiosity. This includes fierce compassion. My intuitive adult awakens within and suddenly being polite is no longer the goal. This situation is asking for boundaries.

Finally, there is a compromise, and we manage to come to an agreement.

"Everyone onto the buses with your yoga mats," I assert.

The buses transport our group to the starting point destination for one of the most renowned sections of the Larapinta at Ormiston Pound Gorge, a place of deep cultural significance.

Dry riverbeds are carved against the sculpted rock formations between ghost gums lining an outdoor art gallery. These red rocks breathe with an intensity, a sensation of the ancient, that I've never felt in an organic landscape before. The gorge has an unnerving magnetism and unknown depth, where sunlight dances cheerfully off the surface of the dark water. The air is struck by the shrill of cicadas. It's sharp and piercing and cuts through our chattering voices with a resounding ring of attention.

Two wedge-tailed eagles circle overhead. Like sovereign presences guarding the 'all' below, they are the original creators that the word 'creature' originates from. Bunjil, steeped in significance as our national totem, symbolises the messengers of our ancestors. Just as protective birds defend their nest, eggs and potential prey, our charming creature may also resist or feel shy when we know we're about to get closer to the truth and reach more profound levels of love and connection. Fear, angst and nervousness come to the surface, ready to be set free like the huge wingspans above. I can sense this amongst the group as we disembark and start to make our way towards our own nest of golden eggs. In our unique ways, we let ourselves be known to the ancestors and silently share our positive intentions for entering the sacred place. Moving in single file, we arrive in the gorge and its beauty reveals itself as an effortless natural amphitheatre.

I hear a person murmur, 'Holy shit.'

We're in the presence of something immense. It is an ageless reality. The power is contained in the land which the Traditional Owners never lost contact with. Only, they knew the stories as we remained visitors, or perhaps even intruders, on a sacred site where listening was the only language available for us to speak.

I don't know it at the time, but that morning, I proceed to teach the most memorable breathwork class I have ever experienced. We begin by laying down our yoga mats in a semicircular shape, half in the sun and half filtered by the shade of the trees above. After setting up the group, I catch my breath and look out across the scene—a spread of humans on a surrounding canvas. Without words, we attune to the breath as a way to connect into the energy and the ceremonial atmosphere. The sand is vibrating with such buzz beneath our mats it could swallow us whole in this utter eeriness which beauty can sometimes emit. As I begin instructing, it doesn't take long for all twenty people to start breathing in unison, filling their chests with pulsating life.

"Begin to merge your inhale with your exhale and connect the breath," I instruct.

Each inhale takes in such fresh, potent air that sweeping energising sparks are sent around a singular field of light.

For the next forty-five minutes, I speak whatever intuitive guidance is coming straight out of the earth and sky. Information hits me in tsunami fashion, with waves of words pouring out of my mouth.

"I trust that my breath is wise and healing."

"What is true beyond my belief that I'm not enough?"

"What is true beyond my perceptions of lack?"

"Perfection no longer serves me. I choose to give up the fight for approval."

The messages from, call them spirit birds, are instructing this class to return to their true source of power.

While everyone has their eyes closed and is immersed fully in their inner world, the eagles are joined by a flock of green, trilling budgies which fly back and forth over the group. It's the most spectacular scene, and I'm in awe, trying to focus on the task at hand while at the same time wanting to prostrate on the ground in sincere thanks, because what else does one do when worshipping this outdoor church?

Awe is a humbling force. It immediately shuts down my animal survival brain, and my monkey mind is replaced by a present focus. My attention on the waves of breath moving in unison round the group creates a kind of collective effervescence. Synchronising our devoted lungs, we pull on imaginary heart strings, playing a harmonious tune composed of all our triumphs and all our tragedies. I remember what my teacher once said to me, "Tina, just open up and be the vessel for awe. If you get out of your own way, magic happens." So, I open and spread my arms like giant wings, hugging the group and begin translating each unique, soul-filled communication. Some come from loved ones who have passed, some from future versions of ourselves, all thrilled that we are amplifying this experience by surrendering fully to it.

Like a grief-quake, the quicksand begins to pull the sadness out of our chests and bodies, dragging the emotions down to the core of the earth where molten lava transmutes any pain into pure power. Breathe far enough into sorrow, and tears turn to sighing, to relief, to gratitude, to laughing and then back into shared air. I watch as everyone is pulled apart and put back together like rising mountains towards the heavens, breath after breath. Naturally taking in and letting go, the longing for all things is at once released to the great mother. After what feels like five minutes, a whole hour passes, and I sense the completion of this process. Everybody has just undertaken a mini hero's journey and a story arc that has healed and restored a sense of peace and blissful emptiness to their organs. Afterwards, we eventually all come to a vertical seat and form a circle, enabling us all to see one another with nobody in front or behind. Every single woman and man shares and speaks out loud the experience that asked for their most vulnerable parts to be exposed.

Human beings need to talk, to be heard, to be witnessed. They need validation of their time, epiphanies, and unspoken empathy, with no interruption or attempt to give advice, fix or counsel. Just seeing the nods around the circles and the fearless gazes of compassion are enough to offer the miracle of transcendence.

"Fuck yes," are the two most spiritual words uttered that day. Every single person recognises their own experience in the other.

Breath can neither be created nor destroyed as it continues on its rebirth journey. It is not possible without a squeezing physical death or the extinction of ancient reptilian fearful thoughts that try to control us. Some of us decide to get on our feet and walk it off silently as we ascend up the hill towards the hiking trail in quietude. Others choose to be still, and sit by the water while the panoramic view comforts and cocoons us.

In a few days, we'll be back in a world of technology, text messages and time frames, but for now there's nothing else to do except breathe and follow the ancient footsteps of the desert's original custodians and charming creatures.

"Communal grieving offers something that we cannot get when we grieve by ourselves. Through validation, acknowledgement and witnessing, communal grieving allows us to experience a level of healing that is deeply shared."

—Sobonfu

Khalil Gibran wrote, *"The deeper that sorrow carves into your being, the more joy you can contain."* Unexpressed emotion becomes a blockage to experiencing the fullness of being a human body contained within a soul. Sigmund Freud says, *"Unexpressed emotions will never die. They are buried alive, and will come forth later, in uglier ways."* It comes down to this: When we aren't given the opportunity, or permission, to grieve our losses, we become stuck—personally and collectively. Our spirits leave our bodies. Disempowerment and depression begin to settle in—and we become a slave to our addictions. We end up living in a kind of endless desert.

It's in this ceremonial way of healing circles that we have remembered our humanity. Evolution always happens in community.

The word spiritual comprises two words we are familiar with ... 'Spiral' and 'Ritual'. Both are aspects of community. Our personal growth and evolution may be compared to a spiral staircase, and rituals are traditions of community.

The ritual of gathering in a group to connect and share unique experiences is profound. It is in this group energy that we invite every emotional state to be witnessed in the recognition that we are not alone in our humanity. No story, emotion or feeling is repressed or rejected. This is both a relief and a responsibility to offer it all up to others as a gift.

In Brené Brown's book, *"Atlas of the Heart"*, she outlines eighty-seven of the emotions and experiences that define what it means to be human. These can include regret, frustrations, despair, anguish, resentment, worry, shame, humiliation, doubt, guilt, longing, sadness, grief and heartbreak.

Francis Weller said it perfectly, *"Grief work offers us a trail leading back to the vitality that is our birthright. When we fully honour our many losses, our lives become more fully able to embody the wild joy that aches to leap from our hearts into the shimmering world."*

The work is holding the mirror up to the group, while seeing your own reflection mirrored back to you without judgement. It is an ancient remembering that cultures across the world have been demonstrating for thousands of years in communities. Evolving is, in essence, not so much a practice as it is the entire force of our deepest nature, our primal need to develop self-realisation and not walk it alone. It is this impulse and longing towards our intuition that is the spiritful journey. As we turn towards our emotional health, we learn that every emotion is simply energy in motion, and part of our body, mind, spirit, soul template of living our intuition. How many times have you had a gut instinct or emotional response about something, and you've chosen to ignore it? What guidance are you getting that you are not listening to?

You know how uncomfortable it feels because your body tells you. You get a knot in your stomach, a headache, a tight lower back, a clenching jaw. The emotional energy you bring into the room with you is more valuable than anything you could think or believe. Acknowledging that we can feel one another's energy helps us understand how much power there is in our own field.

The 'Triskelion'

The three spiralled symbol, the 'Triskelion' will model our spiritful journey together. It is a traditional ancient Greek symbol that represents the power of three, and commonly illustrates the significance of birth, death and rebirth. It celebrates the threefold nature of the Goddess or the Divine Feminine: maiden, mother and crone. It also contains the familiar *body mind spirit* template. It is an integrative model of wholeness and evolution that shows what the ancients knew all along. Everything is connected and we heal in community, not in isolation. These spirals, when bunched together, remind us that 'we are all just walking each other home', as Ram Dass says.

In the middle of this symbol, the soul is placed. The goal of the *soul* is always to bring your health back to balance, to centre you and keep you alive. It is also the home of your intuition and the centre of all truth. When we first visit a yoga mat or meditation cushion, we often are driven by discontent or some form of physical or emotional suffering. We may have made the connection already that when our mind is stressed, we feel pain in our body. Or, when I'm racing, I don't remember who I am or what I like. Or, when my breath is shallow, I'm suffocating with anxiety in my lungs. Or, when I suppress my anger and ignore the intuitive guidance to take action, I stay depressed and unmotivated.

Dr Joe Dispenza states, *"When hard emotions move to moods, move to temperaments, and then to personality traits, we have successfully conditioned the body to live in the past."* In order to create change, we need to move the energy out of the hardened habitual patterns that become concretised in our tissues. Watch a child when they experience disappointment, fear, frustration, or anger. They emote completely ... and then they're finished. Where dysfunction arises is when we get stuck in the washing machine of a negative thinking loop or grieving process. It is unimaginably terrifying to face what wants to be seen and heard inside us, but if we want to be free, do we have a choice? Vulnerability invites the first doorway to healing, which is humility. If I accept my ordinariness, I can be defenceless instead of shielded.

Our initial reaction when life knocks on the back door of our hearts is to run, isolate, mock, mask up, gossip, pretend we don't care, distract by 'doing' and start giving orders to ourselves and others like a controlling teacher. It's a strange thing that the closer we get to any sort of therapy, the louder the ego becomes to avoid the vulnerability. Soon, however, we start to see another path to reduce suffering. One path is called softening into receiving the divine feminine so we can move beyond our past. Stopping people pleasing and picking ourself back up again is a practice we get to participate in over and over again. You know it's your time, when your pain-point returns like an old friend, begging for an embrace. When did you last receive this mercy?

I have a stabbing wound at the back of my heart. It's a nerve raw from both an old and current chronic condition, timeless really. When it flared up last week, my intuition told me, *'Try cupping the sides of your face with the palms of your hands, gently smile, take six conscious breaths, and see if you can stay mad at yourself or someone else.'* Our facial fascia is connected to our pericardium, which protects the heart. Softening our face trickles down and opens things. Exhale. Then listen to what our soul needs at this time.

The heart is not a storage unit. It's an electric, pulsating organism, looking for your love and kindness.

We are going to explore the layers of us and see the *fullness* of their interconnectedness through this *body, mind, spirit, soul* manifesto.

A Spirit *full* Manifesto

BODY

Meet your physical body as its own mini-Earth. Have you ever considered your body as your Earth? Your first home?

Embodying our divine truth, we are all born pure souls, incarnating onto this Earth-realm in physical form.

The word humility comes from the Latin root humus. It means 'to be down low', to be of the Earth, to be on the ground. To be in your body. Grounding into your body is your priority and you begin by paying attention to its intelligence.

Your body is a piece of nature and, therefore, tells you the truth. Its messages are often the opposite to what your mind tells you.
Through the body, we develop reverence for the cycles of change: birth, death, transformation and renewal.

We comprise the same elements as the Earth. We are air, water, earth, and fire, which is pretty amazing. Remember, it is all temporary and constantly changing. The sky grants us perspective, the sun's warmth and fire fosters transformation, the water's essence brings us flow and purification, and the earth reminds us of our grounded, abundant nature.

Our body is where we build a foundation for safety and belonging. Like any ecosystem, it's also our first community, worthy of tending to with care and building a relationship with. Without this steady trust, we can't bring ideas into form or heal an illness.

Coming home requires three things:
- Acceptance
- Surrender
- Humility

Humility is the antidote to victim consciousness. Humility builds a spiritual backbone and encourages you to stand tall and safe in the seat of yourself, no matter what anyone else thinks. You can't embody your intuition if you are weighed down with self-pity or entitlement. Humility dissolves our differences and that has huge value.

> Nick Cave writes, "Humility amounts to an understanding that the world is not divided into good and bad people, but rather it is made up of all manner of individuals, each broken in their own way, each caught up in the common human struggle and each having the capacity to do both terrible and beautiful things. If we truly comprehend and acknowledge that we are all imperfect creatures, we find that we become more tolerant and accepting of others' shortcomings and the world appears less dissonant, less isolating, less threatening."

Our bodies are events in history. Things do not merely happen to us. They happen through us. Our spirit shapes our cell tissue and bone structure, moulding us like clay, like an informant or conductor instructing each noted atom to be sung inside.

The body holds onto many people, jobs, responsibilities and agendas and so, with this awareness, we put it all down and allow ourselves to merge with the planetary body and all creatures being held by greater mother-earthly arms.

MIND

Taoist philosopher Lau Tzu was known for these words, *"To the mind that is still, the whole universe surrenders which is the gift that this layer offers us on the path."* This is about shifting out of the noisy thoughts in our heads and releasing the negative beliefs and stories in our subconscious minds that dictate our choices and habits. I imagine that I am cleaning out the closets of my mind, washing away old wounds, and freeing my inner archive of negative narratives I no longer want to hear.

All the built-up debris and dust must be emptied. Your nervous system can begin to take out the toxicity when you release the anxiety and fears stored in your subconscious body. The fear driven by your egoic mind expresses itself as physical pain, suppressed emotions, anxious thoughts and a continual feeling of being 'tired and wired'. Notice the fears that arise as resistance as a sign you are ready to release these subconscious programs or personal lies.

We often talk about filling our cup, but before we can even consider that, we need to clean it out of all the stuff we have been holding onto. We have to wash the dishes before we make a cuppa. Between the stories of our past traumas, all the emotions that were never processed and all that is happening in the world, we are often overflowing with information. Living in this state of fullness is not optimal or supportive of our intuitive health. If we cling to what is known and comfortable, we get stuck between the cycles and stages of growth. Our energy channels get blocked, our emotions unbalanced and the mind takes over with limiting ruminating thoughts. When we acknowledge and own that we are stuck and actually allow ourselves to feel this way rather than pretending, we are honouring our true selves. Cleaning up our subconscious mind frees us from the reactions of being confused, defensive, judgemental or protective. We have to 'become empty' in order to see clearly for the first time.

Throughout this book, you will receive a roadmap of breathwork practices to empty out the mental body.

SPIRIT

Once we have emptied out, we begin to remember and feel the flow of our own spirit. It feels like energy flowing through us like water when we become present to it. Our spirit is the very essence of who we are. It is our breath, and it's the engine that drives our mind and body. Within our energetic field or spiritual anatomy is intelligent information which informs our physical cells how to behave and what to form. Everything is energy before it becomes matter, which means when we connect to this energy we receive wisdom, intuition and truth to deliver into form Earth-side.

Your spirit is relentless in nudging you to 'listen' to your gifts.
You may have experienced deep spiritual depressions and anxiety when you chose to ignore or sabotage the callings from your spirit. This is often a result of past traumas and contortions in the field that are still influencing your nervous system.

The invitation here is to enter into silence and listen deeply to how your intuition communicates with you. Whether it's through visions, bodily sensations, hearing an inner voice or simply a knowing, when you open yourself to receiving, it's often with a lot less drama than the mental voice.

Sacred listening is hearing 'below' your head. It is the practice of listening without an agenda. You will feel nudges towards a certain truth or clarity around a decision as waves of intuition, and from there creative insights flow.

In chapter five, you learn the different kinds of intuition I refer to as 'waves' and how they communicate with you. It becomes the work of the inner mystic to discern when you are in a flow state and when you aren't. Be quiet and listen.

SOUL

The soul is what survives the death of the body, mind and spirit. You are born into this world through all dimensions with a personal mission and expression that will touch the lives of many and become your legacy.

At this stage, it is becoming clear what soul contract or dharma is guiding your higher purpose. Your soul is also imprinted with archetypal patterns which are completely unique to you and are a big clue as to why certain things excite one person but bore another. By now, you have experienced that asking your soul what it wants is not a comfortable question for your ego. When this discomfort and fear arises, you invite your future wise woman to expand and take up more space without apology. It's not about switching off your reasoning mind and intellect, but rather, creating a partnership moving forwards and learning to discern the difference between those two voices.
You will learn the difference between the voice of fear and the voice of love. Practically, it's much simpler than you might believe.
This is a compassionate partnership where your ego serves your soul and its mission to be of service to others.

PRACTICE MEDITATION

Intuitive Mountain Meditation

This meditation practice supports our energy by connecting our body, mind, spirit, and soul as one ecosystem.

We strengthen our alignment with Earth by widening the base of our mountain, so that the peak can go higher. It's the same principles of physics that make a pyramid. Big base equals higher peak. When we are guided to stay steady and push our roots deep down, we have more potential to ascend upwards. The law of correspondence states *'as above, so below'*, therefore, we are aligned both with the energies of Source in the higher heavens and with the earthly energies of the grounded mountain.

1. *Find a comfortable upright seat and close your eyes, resting the backs of your hands on your thighs with palms facing upwards.*

2. *Imagine you are in your favourite place in nature. Imagine that your body is a mountain in this place. Your sit bones are connected to the Earth. Your legs form the base of the mountain. Your arms are the sides of the mountain. And your head is the top of the mountain with your crown forming the peak. You are sturdy and strong and have been here for millions of years. Feel your whole bone structure creating the shape of this mountain in its unique way.*

3. *Imagine your thoughts are like clouds. They drift around the top of the mountain. Every thought is a different cloud with a different shape and texture, some light and some heavy. You don't need to identify with the clouds. Simply witness them.*

4. *Imagine your breath is like the wind. Take three deep conscious breaths and listen to the sound of your own wind filling your lungs. Imagine with each breath that you can blow the clouds*

away. Gently, they float and change form and disappear and dissolve.

5. *Imagine your spirit is the sky. This vastness of the day and the night wraps around the mountain and forms a backdrop. Just like the sky, your spirit is limitless and unbound. It stretches beyond the horizon and is a field of energy that is alive with information, vibration and colours.*

6. *Now imagine at the very centre of your mountain is your soul. Right in your heart centre is a fire, and it is the core of your knowing. Bring your awareness to this warmth and follow the longing. Allow the heat to spread across your chest and fill up your mountain body with charm and unconditional love.*

7. *An illumination is erupting from inside you as a vision that is surfacing, which once was covered by fear but is now becoming clear. The Buddhists describe this as 'Bodhicitta' or the eternal essence that will not die. This insight supports you and you are being asked to honour it. Attune to your core any time you feel like you have drifted away from your truth and need to discover the next step on your pilgrimage.*

How am I nourishing my *Intuitive Mountain*?

CHAPTER 4

ALCOHOL IS NOT RUINING MY LIFE BUT I CAN'T STOP DRINKING

Which woman am I?

There's a rogue woman in my head. The instant I wake, the story begins. My mind editing like the spellcheck function on computer. Scanning, autocorrecting and looking for flaws.

I am here. In my bed. Good wife. Adequate mother. Sufficient pet owner. Hard worker. Devoted yogi. Committed woman who always tries her best and starts each day positively. Ugh, my neck is stiff. Too much stress. Probably haven't stretched enough. Chest feels heavy. Can't seem to suck in enough air. What kind of Zen yoga teacher am I if I can't even breathe? What's wrong with me?

And just like that, with my horizontal thinking, the world gets made.

Or a movie gets made?

I do this movie-making in my mind to survive. My prefrontal cortex is constantly searching for patterns of recognition for familiarity and certainty. Like an IT virus software, it seeks the same algorithms so it can stay one step ahead of the present moment, sifting out the truth to present me with a whole lot of false 'safe' options.

Who is this trying to survive and get out of bed?

'I' am.

The lead character in my own movie, 'I' starts to narrate incessantly and mistakes the reality I've made with my thoughts for the real world. This identity believes all its past projections are fact and starts acting on them.

I am registering the chores I need to do and hop out of my car hastily to walk towards the supermarket with bag in hand. Moving through the sliding doors, a feeling rushes around my tightened shoulders, caused by conflict between my brain and my heart.

Should I turn left, or should I turn right?

The left side of the supermarket is a wall of colourful alcoholic liquids, crafted with attractive, non-threatening wine labels shaping the architecture of the bottle shop shrine.

The right is everything else.

My head says ... *definitely left, without question. Don't be uncomfortable today. Just enjoy this Monday as an opportunity to ease into the week with a nice new flavour of Rosé. You deserve it. Live like a French sommelier would. Go easy on yourself.*

My heart says ... *you don't need this today, Tina. Your body wants a chance to love you and show you how intelligent it is at creating space, energy and getting rid of toxic stinking thinking. You will gain so much clarity and sleep better if you turn right. Rest is very important, and I have some important messages to channel to you from Source that will blow your mind and expand your soul. Let's create a new reality together! Drink water instead.*

I turn left.

My shoulders slump forwards and my bones take on the shape of shame as I open the fridge door to grab a bottle of wine. Placing it into my basket, I then proceed to quickly grab all the other things for the weekly meals so I can get home and enable myself. My breath gets caught in my chest and I open my mouth to grab some extra air. Dammit, rogue woman is winning, and intuition is losing.

As I walk towards the checkout, I run into a local friend who greets me with a smile and a chance to chat. She has come to my community yoga classes in the past and shares with me her latest wellness practices and weight-loss achievements. Self-conscious of my basket contents, I move a bushy bunch of parsley over the top of the bottle to conceal that I'm about to pour poison down my throat on a Monday while wearing unmistakeable Lululemon active wear.

I wonder in that moment how I would communicate to her if I chose to turn right. I might be standing a bit taller, my eyes bright and wide, my words strong and deliberate, my spirit full and lively. Full of vigour.

Not the 'I' running the show, but the charming creature believing in herself.

I do have two charming creatures inside me. One is a fast, jumpy fieldmouse, and the other is a big plodding elephant.

Upon waking, I often pose the question ... *which creature will I feed today? The mouse or the elephant?*

My honest charming creature of the elephant, wanting to guide the true path, is the one I need to nurture. It embodies intuition and is highly intelligent. The one I must feed with a devoted spiritful practice and daily stillness. The elephant finds security from within and doesn't need to seek approval from others. It knows who it is, what it wants and is safe in the seat of itself. Steady, grounded and unshakeable.

The mouse represents a boundary-less distraction and can squeeze through the tiniest of spaces in my psyche if I'm not awake to it. That it can hide in my subconscious makes it skilful at pulling me out of the moment. I can react urgently and too fast when what is required is pausing and responding. I can be arrogant enough to believe I must do it all perfectly because nobody else will do the job as well. I crave to be many places at once, breeding myself into burnout.

Looking at Ganesha, the elephant in Hindu mythology, he uses the mouse as his mode of transport, symbolising triumph over the ego. The ego is neither good nor bad, but a necessary part of this existence to transcend and awaken consciousness. Ganesha's wise, mindful and slow determination means it sees the mouse for what it is; a survival default mode which comes with its humanness.

Which part of myself do I want or need to nourish more? And why?

Once we make this conscious, we discover there's not just two, but a whole zoo of charming creatures inside our minds. Some nurture our creative genius and others ensure we cross the road without getting hit by a car. I have tried to starve the storied self and shovel food into the more evolved wise self, but it often meant I felt split or torn. The key is not to starve one and feed the other, but to befriend them all into belonging. To befriend them both into wholeness.

Belonging to all solves the predicament of the ego's perceived separation and includes the truth that we can own our complexity. We can own both our light and our shadow. Maybe this is what Noah was trying to do when he built his arc. Include the entire kingdom and allow them to learn to live with each other as we tend to the different creatures' needs.

"We all have an edge. We all are floating our psyche on top with a great ocean underneath."

—Brad Dourif

Alcohol is not ruining my life, but I can't stop drinking.

It's the problem without having an actual problem.

I hope you're comforted to hear you're not alone and that we all have a rogue woman living inside our heads governing our automated, addictive decisions. My life is healthy and thriving. It has not imploded. But I would like to experience days, weeks, and months without always returning to this habit energy. According to the status quo, if you are an alcoholic, you are dysfunctional, and the rest of society can drink responsibly because they stick to the two standard drinks per day. So, in other words, if you're not a train wreck and drinking before noon, then there's no problem?

We have been fed a false story by those who are capitalising off this habit and popular social acceptance. The arrogant assumption is that drinkers are the normal ones and anyone who is not is weird, pregnant, not to be trusted, or training for a triathlon.

When you refuse a drink, the crowd tends to stare at you suspiciously like you're either a complete buzzkill or mentally unwell, and no one knows what to do with either of those. It feels easier in social situations to pin this counter-cultural decision on an excuse like "I'm on antibiotics" than to simply say "I don't drink". For a while, I simply withdrew from gatherings or functions, knowing it would cost me friendships and traditions. But strangely, what came about was new ways of connecting, and lots of walking.

Alcohol is very misunderstood as a substance. It's a known depressant drug. For women in their forties, it's like pouring petrol on top of a cocktail of fluctuating peri-menopausal hormones. It hurts my body. Fogs my mind. Dampens and drains my spirit. Conflicts with my soul. A habit that does this cannot be truly spiritual. Or can it?

I became sober curious, and it led to some very inconvenient truths. I toyed with on-again, off-again experiments but never lasted longer than a few months. I would do forty days in a row alcohol free, then fifty days, 'Feb fasts' and retreat detoxes, and finally when those periods were over, the habit would creep back in like a skilled ninja. Especially at night. Ninjas see well in the dark and seem to connect with my shadows when my defences are down and I'm tired from a long day. A glass of wine a night becomes the new normal again, justified by a busy survival brain. I would even fill my glass with ice cubes in the hope that the extra hydration would dilute my shame and water down my negative judgemental self-talk. At some point, I tell myself a story which allows this behaviour to continue. I'm either listening to an unconscious narrative or I'm listening to my intuition which is saying ... *you are addicted to alcohol, Tina. There are healthier ways to ease discomfort and take the edge off.*

Eventually though, I'd pay attention to the voice telling me I need to make more caring choices. I didn't enjoy my relationship with alcohol anymore. It no longer felt true or kind. I'm no stranger to addiction. I was dependent on opioids for three years, in chronic pain and craving constant numbness through self-medication. The numbing of pain and the numbing of joy at the same time. Impossible to separate with the blanket of anaesthesia.

The early years of motherhood invited another dimension of drinking to fit in with the 'Mummy Wine culture' at bath time. Take a sip, turn on the tap. Take a sip ... *when will my husband be home?* Take a sip ... *how long till bedtime?*

I don't identify as an alcoholic, though. Surely, I haven't suffered enough if I'm only consuming one drink each day. It does not feel authentic to say I'm an alcoholic because I don't binge drink or wake up hungover, and yet, I am still seeking something, a feeling, a permission slip, a reprieve from the perceived stressors, an edge buster.

How did we become so binary over this addiction?

This experiment has shown that this is not about the alcohol at all. It's about the choice to take on your intuition. Which voice will you act on?

The voice of the rogue woman or the voice of the wise woman?

Most likely you are granting the rogue woman way too much power.

When I'm present and awake to the rogue woman, I'll often challenge her and ask her to reveal what it is she's hiding from me.

Most often, she wants me to stay unconscious, so I don't have to feel uncomfortable emotions.

The more we choose our intuition, the stronger it becomes. Like a muscle. The higher our self-esteem ascends as we prove that we can count on ourselves to support our own cravings. What is required is a complete rethinking of addiction. The invitation is to shift our attention from the addiction to the craving and enquiring into why we want to disconnect from numbing our intuitive hearts in the first place. Once I let go of the strong painkiller drug dependence, more culturally accepted ones took their place. Social media, work, online shopping, obsessing over beauty and anti-aging trends, and co-dependent relationships. All served their purpose to numb emotional discomfort and control the outside world.

Your addiction may be as obvious in your life as a thunderstorm—the damage clear as day to you as it is to everyone around you. Or yours may be a quiet internal cyclone that no one knows about. Not even your friends. Not even your partner sleeping beside you in bed.

The substance or behaviour becomes irrelevant when you dig a bit deeper, as they are all trying to achieve the same thing. Avoiding fear and shame. The spiritual masters say in the end, you'll be able to free yourself from your addictive patterns 'as smoothly as drawing a hair from a slab of butter'. Until then, you swing between grief and gratitude. Grief because you realise the waste of your old ways, and gratitude because you feel the joy that gives birth to a new profound power that you're no longer in prison.

In *"The Wisdom of No Escape",* Buddhist nun Pema Chodron wrote, *"Life is a whole journey of meeting your edge again and again. That's where, if you're a person who wants to live, you start to ask yourself questions like, 'Now, why am I so scared? What is it that I don't want to see? Why can't I go any further than this?'"*

What is the truth we don't want to hear?

What are we unwilling to feel?

Stopping the war within me required a spiritual transformation of radical honesty. I'd like to be free from the running urge to numb, but in order to do that, I need to lean into the discomfort.

Just like alcohol (or insert your addiction of choice), spiritual practices such as meditation can also be used to bypass our hard emotions such as grief, shame and anger. This spiritual bypassing creeps up on devotees who become hooked on altered states of consciousness. A definite shadow side to the surrendered flow state of intuition exists, which we'll discuss in the next chapter. It's interesting to deepen this enquiry into what my charming creature desires, not as right or wrong or good or bad, but more a pull towards greater authenticity and alignment. I'm not interested in judging anyone for their choices around alcohol, food, or any other substance. I am interested in revealing that you have the capacity to act on your own truth. You have the power to choose what feels hard but is your ultimate calling in life.

Self-sabotage is not just addiction to things we put in our mouth. It's also our addiction to wanting attention, recognition, co-dependency and martyrdom. Even if the shadow saboteur leads us down some dark pathways, it ultimately is the catalyst for our spiritful awakenings.

The saboteur is wired into the human condition and mostly wants to be befriended rather than berated in order to heal it. The saboteur is the voice known as the 'inner critic' and is not our true intuitive voice. We know we're really gaining traction in our life when our inner critic gets abusive and attempts to keep us stuck in our comfort zone. It looks for external threats and soothes its fear from the outside in instead of the inside out.

Compassion and care are the medicine it needs to reverse its relationship with power, and to trust that you are well resourced within to support its recovery. Speak kindly to your addictive voice because it's the part of you that's scared, hypervigilant and just trying to protect you.

Over time, we become so exhausted and worn down from listening to our saboteur that we begin to seek refuge and recovery. To be in recovery is to recover a part of yourself that's been tied down from meeting the edge because that part has been so busy 'taking the edge off'. The view of life from the edge of life is different to the view from the non-edge. Hunter S Thompson wrote of going to one's edge, *"The Edge ... There is no honest way to explain it because the only people who really know where it is are the ones who have gone over."* These times are calling for us to explore ourselves beyond where we've been comfortably plonked (pardon the pun). It's our willingness to peer over, to tip the balance and freefall through the layers of ourselves, through the collective crises, and to find new ground. Pressing the easy escape button of alcohol is the safe and serene centre. Taking yourself on rebelliously is the messy and edgy button which we're invited to enter.

Can you think of a moment in your daily life where it's an opportunity to meet your edge? The edge is the point where you dare to do something different than your habitual routine.

> Will you turn the hot water in the shower to cold and stand under it for a minute?
>
> Will you drink herbal tea instead of coffee?

Will you meditate in bed before rushing to get up at sunrise?

Will you have a difficult conversation with a family member about boundaries?

Will you read a book before picking up your phone at night?

Our courage to evolve and extend ourselves beyond habit energy is our commitment to being spiritful. The shock of leaping off an edge rather than taking the edge off can be shockingly confronting. It's a bit like when you are in a nightclub and they turn on the closing time lights at 3.00 am. There's no hiding when the illusion of smoke and mirrors has been revealed.

You grab onto the edge and crawl back to the old version of you and her habits because it's so unexpected when every ghost from your childhood rocks up to the dance party all at the same time. This is why it is best not to go alone, or to at least find a buddy or your own circle of addiction sisters to be the parachutes. Together, you'll find a suitable replacement for the habit energy. It might be an evening walk, swim, writing partner or sunrise meditation.

Recovery means to salvage, rescue or reclaim. It is like a pilgrimage or a vision quest in which we journey through our inner landscape. Sometimes we do this while journeying through an actual physical landscape or well-known trail in another country. Either way, it requires inner work and the reclamation to become whole and spiritful and more like the person we were born to be. The edge of things is the best place to live as it's here where we get to know the sensitive, kind, funny, brave and wise women we are.

Overall, it's been this gradual tapering and letting go that has made my anguish dissolve. Will I go full sober? Perhaps. Perhaps not. For now, the edge is where it's at.

"Listen, are you breathing just a little and calling it a life?"

—Mary Oliver

PRACTICE MEDITATION

One Breath Meditation

The following meditation is all about guiding you to experience the power of one conscious breath. It's not a breathwork class. It's not about the quantity of breaths that you take, which is actually about 20,000 breaths per day. This meditation is to connect you back into the power of one full conscious breath. It's about the quality of breath, not quantity.

1. *Let's begin by finding a comfortable seat. Settle yourself in with your back nice and straight. You might be at home, parked in the car, sitting at the desk. Wherever you are, this five-minute meditation is going to take you back to a place of connection. Now, close down your eyes and just relax your hands and your shoulders. Begin by taking one big inhale through the nose and an exhale out the mouth with a sigh, letting yourself land in this moment. Give yourself this little pocket of time to journey inwards. Notice how the breath is showing up in your body. Just observe where you feel it without any effort. Notice where it might be moving, whether that's in your belly, your spine, your chest, your nostrils. Just feel how the breath is showing up.*

2. *Picture or imagine in your mind's eye behind your forehead an image of a mountain. We all know the shape of a mountain. Imagine that with your pointer finger, you're going to trace the outline of the mountain, starting at the base, allowing your finger to travel up towards the peak and then down the other side, back to the base of the mountain. Now take your next conscious breath and imagine it moving like the shape of that mountain as you inhale, bringing the breath all the way up towards the peak. Notice how the breath moves down the other side of the mountain, inching your lungs all the way to the base, all the way to its completion. Notice that this is one complete breath.*

You're not starting halfway up the mountain. You're not beginning at the top and falling down. You're not going backwards. You are taking one conscious breath at a time. Every moment that you find your mind wanders, or you get distracted by thought, or you feel pain in your body, or you can sense something pulling you away, come back to that image of the mountain and take one conscious breath, beginning at the base and following it all the way to its completion. It's just one quality breath. Again, if you get distracted or in your head, just return to one complete mountain breath.

3. *The practice is the returning, not saying that you have nothing to achieve or strive for here. You are not aiming for many mountains. You are simply positioning yourself back into a place of power to take one full conscious breath. As you continue to trace the movement of the breath over your mountain, you may notice now that there is a second mountain right beside this mountain. This second mountain is inviting you to consciously now connect your breath to the next inhale. So, the next time your lungs empty of air, you can invite an inhale back in straightaway, like two friends holding hands, standing side by side as these two mountains are. Now imagine that you are tracing the outline of both of them in one fluid motion, inhaling all the way up, consciously connecting the breath.*

4. *Put the palms of your hands down on the thighs, giving them a rub, grounding yourself as the mountain that you are with a beautiful body. Then you'll release the meditation, with one final breath in and out of the mouth, as a sigh. Now you can return to whatever it is you were doing or being. Know you can come back to the power of that one conscious breath at any time, finding some solid ground, something reliable to*

stand and walk on, and perhaps even a little lightness in your step.

BIG LITTLE SISTER STORY
TUULI VIKSTEDT

Yoga retreat. A bunch of weird Western wannabes prancing around in their harem pants and hairy armpits drinking detox smoothies. A few years ago, that's pretty much how I would have, rather scientifically, defined 'retreat'. Growing up worrying about basic needs and then dedicating my life to worrying about ensuring basic needs for others, I saw yoga retreats as a product of too much wealth and wellbeing—some enlightened (entitled) nonsense directed to those who already had everything in life to go and dwell on all the nothing. How could anyone justify starving themselves with spirulina while others were living in famine without safe drinking water? My sceptic soul saw nothing 'alkaline' about that ...

I have always loved yoga and enjoyed it as part of my exercise regime. Then came children, and all democracy and free will of my yogic realm got pretty much swept off the mat. Between breastfeeds, it suddenly became easier—and more tempting—to run out the door and leap around the gardens than book in a downward-facing dog at a studio. In fact, so much did I enjoy the adrenaline, and the guilty pleasure of escaping the toddler town, that I ended up running a whole marathon—with the postnatal pelvic floor strength of a ripe plum and abdominal separation wider than fjords. Eventually, it took one fortuitous book launch at a Mother's Day lunch with one beautifully grounded author to pull me back in alignment. Now looking back, returning to the mat with Tina was clearly the "Mother's Medicine" my mind and body had been craving for. A book, by the way, that is still one of the best and bravest books I've read.

Of course, I had known (of) Tina before. She was the soft, mystical creature who I regularly saw floating in and out of school drop-offs and pickups, with a step so light it looked like she was elevating on feathers. Our kids shared a school but as she's a 'girls' mum' and I'm a 'boys' mum', our worlds never mingled much. As anyone with school-aged children would know, the two motherly species rarely mix as we don't tend to share the same courts around kids' sport and gossip.

I loved her Yin class instantly. Her classes dive right beyond the asanas. Her insanely funny storytelling. Wisdom mixed with wit and giggles. Her fair dinkum kickass-ness. The unconditional love she fills the room with. And, of course, the occasional and random, yet very well intended, f-bomb. With Tina, I find myself doing yoga not for the exercise nor for any routines, but purely for the wholistic experience she creates. In her guidance, it felt only natural to gingerly proceed towards the world of harem pants. No smoothies.

My love affair for retreats has been a slow burn. After my curiosity was teased open with Tina's Yin, I took the first leap towards retreating with her in 2020. Of course, the COVID lockdowns asked us for a raincheck for the following year. But I had turned forty and felt pretty brave and ready. And who wouldn't feel brave and ready to spend a long weekend in Byron Bay in the most beautiful, lush hinterland estate among like-minded women celebrating midlife vibes—with an enlightened vegan chef? Clear as ghee if you ask me. I chucked my judgement, packed an open mind and leaped out of my (dis)comfort zone—and into my harem pants. Not!

I will always remember the feeling of stepping out of our four-day immersion in the Blue Green Sanctuary. Something in me had shifted. I felt fully refreshed, as if an old, grotty beach towel had gone through a wash cycle with buckets of Fluffy's divine blends. Ecstatic. Fragrant. Light. Aware. And yes—madly awakened. Not necessarily so much for my new spiritual higher self, but for all the love, light, freedom, flow, wild energy, good intention and intuitive insight we got to harvest from Tina's teachings and share in this magical space together. Did I even feel a tiny bit enlightened? Why not! But I very well recall post-retreat reverting back to thinking about basic needs. I concluded that perhaps a good couple of days connecting with open-minded, kind-hearted people, searching inward yet reaching outward should really be a basic need fulfilled for everyone. A few more of us cosmic wannabes would totally make this world a better, more balanced and peaceful place.

From Byron Bay to the Larapinta Trail, all the way up to the mountain trails of the Annapurna's, I've been privileged to see, feel and experience the healing Tina's retreats enable. Since being on her journey now for some years, I can confidently say something in me has shifted. For good this time. I feel like I've learned to receive the world differently. More fluidly. I give much less notice to what society might expect from me or how other people might perceive me. I'm grateful for my new set of lenses, as it hasn't always been an easy vision.

Losing my mum and consequently coping with my dad's mental health at a young age came with stigma. Pitied. Confused. Embarrassed. Later, growing up in a girls' home added further stigma. It was a decent place, like a little bird's nest with beautiful sisters and mothers for life—but we were perceived as losers. As juveniles. In high school, I'm sure I had the same two legs and two arms as every other girl (not to mention my hot ass) but really struggled to find anyone to take me to the prom. Why would anyone want to show up with a girl from the facility? A few years after, as my feathers changed, and I became a world class swan with two university degrees, I established a children's house in Nepal to give back the gift of life and opportunity to disadvantaged children there, and these same judges were truly amazed. How could a girl with nothing actually become something?

I suddenly had a life that became a sought-after Cinderella story in my native Finland. We ended up in newspapers and magazines, no doubt always with the same old spin—look at her pushing off from the dent of desperation and despair. The publicity was very handy for fundraising and lifting our organisation's profile for the children in Nepal, but giving interviews killed me every time—the content was already predetermined, even before I spoke a word. On the other hand, here in Australia, people who don't know my full story are often quite happy for me as I'm able to have this wonderful little 'hobby' in Nepal. Of course, when you are married to an ex-footballer, you get to be a housewife and play a little with philanthropy. How lucky am I?

Sarcasm aside, I do feel very lucky. Since kick-starting my lifelong journey inwards with Tinalina, it's been lovely to notice how other people's stories about my story have become way less interesting to me. More importantly, my own stories of my own story have numbed. Judgement from others—including my own self talk—feels like, if not quite white noise then definitely has all the fifty shades of grey. No colours. Like a gentle fart that pops up, stinks a little and floats away. I'm slowly learning the art of letting go. I'm learning to go easier on life. To go easier on me.

Tuuli Vikstedt
– Co-founder and Director of Wind of Change International

CHAPTER 5
SURF INDO WAVES

I sat with the craving and the need to self soothe. That thirst for alcohol always pretended to be a friend and a reliable crutch. In its absence, I felt a sense of sadness for all the moments I had forgotten and all the joy and sunsets I had numbed. I chose to take hold of my pen instead, and these are the words that flowed out.

I don't remember.

I don't remember how to be free. Can it be as simple as breathing? I don't remember the sand dunes, the wind and the trees. I don't remember the peace that flows like a river through my veins and out my fingertips. I don't remember the melting of a hug or the desire of a kiss. I don't remember all the movies in my head that made up stories and told tales. I don't remember how to jump really high or how to laugh uncontrollably. I don't remember the smoothness of my skin unwrinkled and youthful like pastel and velvet. I don't remember skipping or singing in rounds and rounds.

Will this vessel hold more of my own essence? I don't remember the colour of my essence, but I can feel its tingling. It is inviting and tantalising. The soles of my feet are alive with wonder, but my heart is heavy with worry. Where can these two parts join and merge? Exhaling, I wonder what it would be like to breathe underwater. Like other mammals with giant weighted bodies, be able to float and glide without burden. I imagine being a blue whale with a big-eyed soul.

Calling, calling, calling for a response and a sign that I am catching the correct current. I trust that one day I'll remember these bones are ancient. I don't remember all the lifting they have done, but I feel it. I wish now to be lifted. To rise up and burst through the surface, inhaling the essence of this spark. It is all so brief, so why do I act like it's serious? I don't remember the moment I chose this body and fell from a star to be inside this skin. It may have been very dark, and I was ok with that. Still, I know I started in fluid. I was weightless and buoyant and there was nothing I needed to do but breathe.

"I'm afraid of what is coming," I said to the ocean this morning.

"It's just a wave. Take a breath," the ocean advised.

I am barefoot and paddling through a process of re-discovering my soul's flow so I can remember all the things I knew but need to know again.

Inhaling deeply, I smell the waft of Indonesia pass through my nostrils. Walking along the beach to meet my surf coach for an on-sand lesson, before we head out on the boat, fills me with trepidation.

"Don't look so nervous," he says. "I've taught seventy-year-olds to stand up on their first go."

He doesn't know who he's dealing with. I am a forty-four-year-old leg person. I use my legs a lot to walk, stand, practise yoga and even do the splits. My legs will be my legacy. Born to traverse the land and stay on the well-trodden path, using my arms to paddle is foreign. My arms are like dangling accessories. I am far from a four-limbed creature. Long and thin, they can make great gestures if I am drowning and trying to get a lifesaver's attention, but when it comes to using them like oars, they seek a motor to propel the body forwards.

"Let's pretend the surfboard is a yoga mat," he proposes.

Great. Now he's talking my language.

I lie down on my belly and notice my feet hang over the end.

"Oh, let me get you a longer board. This one is too short for your legs," he says.

"Now, I want you to pretend you are paddling, then tuck your toes, bring your hands under your shoulders and push up into seal pose."

Cool, I'm in a yoga pose, I'm nailing this.

"Are you right-footed or goofy?" he asks.

I've got no idea, but what are the chances I'd be goofy? I bet that with my track record I'm the weirder version.

My left foot naturally jumps forwards first, and he declares, "Yes, you are goofy. Now, once your left foot is on the board, bring your right foot to follow like a warrior pose. Point your right arm out in front and look straight ahead towards your future. Don't look down at your feet. Always forwards."

I take the familiar stance and, on the fat foamy board below, I feel the vibe, trusting the immoveable earth beneath me.

"Alright, you're ready. Let's go get on the boat," he says.

I pick up my board and carry it under my arm like I've done this a hundred times. Confidently walking down to the shore, meeting my family and the other surfers staying at the resort, we load up and settle in for the aquatic fun-ride.

"Checking the weather one final time," he declares. "We're going to Telescopes. The waves there are family-fun-size and easy."

I imagine this section of the surf break is just like the mini chocolate bars. Easily digestible, sweet, and safe for all ages.

As we approach the reef, lots of other boats are anchored around the edges of the seamless rolling waves. The water is smooth and there is absolutely no wind, creating glassy ideal conditions that green rooms are made of and where barrels are dreamed into reality. Waves like blue mountains rise from the horizon and move through a boundless, sequinned sea. These liquid mountains swell with size to toppling peaks and make me gulp.

The boat stops and we're told to jump off while our boards are lowered into the water.

'Jumping off' means diving into the middle of the ocean with no land to stand on, the waves surrendering their strength as they crash on the reef beneath them.

"Start paddling," the teacher instructs, whom I also call God and will not let out of my sight.

I hop on my beginner's longboard and follow my kids and husband who are excited I'm participating and that we're all together.

I don't even notice my arms moving through the water because I'm distracted by the beauty of the sun setting and the colours of the sky. I'm in nature's paradise. The Earth's bath is cleansing me of any fear as I allow the energy and grace of this moment to fill my heart with joy.

"Ok, Tina, follow me over here," the teacher says. "When I see a wave, I'm going to push you onto it, and you'll do exactly as we practised on the beach."

I would be so happy just to lie on my board and soak in the environment like a sea sponge, but before I know it, I hear, "Turn around. We're going for this one!"

"Are you sure? It looks a bit big," I stammer.

My husband bursts into laughter, "It's completely calm."

There is no time to hesitate.

I focus and place all my attention on the present moment. I concentrate and feel myself being propelled forwards with a big whoosh.

Tuck toes. Left foot forwards. And boom, I'm standing. I'm surfing!

I knew I could trust my legs to do it. Maybe it's beginner's luck, but I fully own the sheer shock of the moment and wobble my way along the water.

"Yeeeeew."

Shrieks come from behind me.

"Mum, you did it!"

Cool, a cheer squad of supporters share their thrilled surfie war cries.

As the wave closes in, I fall to the side and feel the yank of the leg rope tug on my ankle as my board goes one way and my body flies in the opposite direction.

My feet look for something solid to stand on but—dammit—I'm on a reef. The coral scrapes my skin as I try to grab the rope and pull my board back towards me. Another wave crashes onto my head. I gasp for air and try to swim towards my board so I have something to hold on to. Another wave shoves me further away. And then another. And another. I'm starting to fatigue and can see the other surfers out the back looking towards me encouragingly. Being stuck in the break zone is not fun. We didn't practise this. I try to stay calm and double down on my yogic breathing.

I gasp at the violent rise and crash of the waves. Water piles in over my head, rushing into my mouth and jetting up my nose.

Bobbing on the surface like a buoy with limbs being thrown in different directions, my eyes are stinging and blurred with salt and all I look for is my board to keep me afloat.

"Why is nobody rescuing me?" I think.

This seems futile. I'm getting nowhere. I long for solid ground and anything still. I cannot believe the power, so much bigger than my own will. I look down now and see blood dripping down my shin. I don't know its source but am conscious of becoming shark bait.

I don't feel like a surfer. I feel like a fish out of water. I'm swimming in foolishness, my courage getting me into big trouble.

It's assumed that when you consent to a surf lesson that you can swim. It would be easier if I could blame someone else for this drowning performance. At least swimming teachers were easy to hate when I was five years old, often strict and uncompromising in their soggy t-shirts. Surf instructors, though, are like labradors. Gorgeous and friendly, they just want to be your best friend so you can experience the spiritual high the secret code of surfers hold.

I realise quickly I need to have a serious conversation with my arms. *Hey guys, if you don't fire up and help me survive here, we are going to drown. Nobody is going to save us. We need to save ourselves. Use your instincts.* Clearly, what feels like an hour is actually less than a minute, just enough time to be 'initiated'. I see some heads turn back and experienced eyes still looking at me encouragingly. If I could hear their thoughts, I imagine them saying, "You can do it, girl. C'mon, dig deeper." And with that, a burst of pure adrenal energy moves my bionic bones like they've never moved before. My hands become the size of hulks, and I grab the board and rotate my shoulders as fast as possible until finally I am beyond the crash zone.

Exhausted, I flop head down and float so I can catch my breath and let the sting in my muscles subside.

"Hey, you're a natural, first time! Let's go again," God, the instructor, exclaims. I don't know whether to hug him or hate him.

Grateful that my body knew exactly what to do when fear fought hard against it, means I learn a new respect for my arms' intuition to act. So wise. Thank you, body.

I felt the flow state and the fear state in the same second.

I don't know if I ever will do that again, but somehow I must find my way back into the water. The salty oceanic power has the answers.

Intuition is the ability to instantly understand or know something without a need to cognitively think about it or use reason to discover it. It's easy to become imprisoned by our own thoughts, pushing from past patterns and over-identifying with responsibility. When we find the courage to move in new ways from the heart, we can expand towards the unknown rather than resist it and cling to control.

Qualities of weightlessness, floating, freedom, softness, buoyancy and surrender continued to beckon me to the shore. Is it a coincidence that the language to describe our experience in the water is also used to talk about spirituality? Is it a coincidence that particles of light are also called waves? Learning to surf these internal waves invites me deeper.

The last few years sent me on an exploration where I found myself submerging my body in the ocean. I needed to feel this power greater than me. I felt the fear when stuck in the break zone, turbulence and the whitewash of anxiety on the surface. I felt the peace and nothingness when suspended deep down in the void of floating space. I felt the joy when surfing in the flow and the wave lifted me up and carried me along without effort. Even though the moments of staying up on a surfboard were few and far between, I became curious that I was in a cycle of waves.

After a decade of studying intuition and doing readings on people, I learned there is not just intuition, but intuitions.

1. **Survival Intuition**
2. **Deep Communion Intuition**
3. **Flow State Intuition**

Survival Intuition is our physical level of intuition. It is our biological 'gut instinct' and is designed to protect us and to keep us safe and alive. This kind of intuition keeps our head above the water and is activated by our fight/flight/freeze response in our nervous system which all animals rely upon to sense danger. It is unconscious and automatic, operating through our vagus nerve, and is our primal nature.

The current. The rip that pulls you out to sea is the force of this intuition that takes you in a direction whether you're ready or not. You can either fight against it and become exhausted from the struggle, or you let it take you out towards a new horizon.

The shadow side of this is when our nervous system becomes chronically activated in a sympathetic response and we find ourselves stuck in a loop of fight/flight/freeze. We begin to make our decisions from anxiety and fear rather than from our higher wisdom. We also attach ourselves to thoughtforms of the ego which pursues its goals in seeking superiority, comparison, scarcity and lack. We become dysfunctional and addicted to our stress hormones.

Deep Communion Intuition is when we sink below the surface of the ocean and enter the void. This is the womb-like stage of submerging. Getting below the noisy whitewash and surface gasping. It's the stage of creating intentional quietude so we can hear and receive the voice of intuition.

I like to combine this sinking with soaking. I've learned how to replicate the ocean in my bathtub by adding a kilo of salt. We are made of salt water and as I feel my body dissolve, I can melt and become one with the truth. This familiar fluid is where an umbilical cord of light plugs me into the cosmic mother, and I receive all the intelligence in the universe simply by existing. There's nothing I need to do or say. In this deep silence and suspension, we awaken a conversation with another voice. We begin to test it out and communicate with it by asking for guidance such as …

Give me a sign.

Show me the next step.

We wait for answers and practise patience, knowing that this relationship needs careful tending to.

The shadow side to being in the deep is that we can get too comfortable in the darkness. We become stuck in our anchors on the ocean floor and too attached to our past beliefs to be able to receive new guidance.

Flow State Intuition happens when we are in present time. We become one with the ocean, immersed in a field beyond time and space. This is also known as being 'in the zone', or channelling, and feels as if time disappears. We are fearless, trusting the energy that is flowing through us. It's like time is flying and the ego falls away, along with its agendas.

Hungarian American psychologist Mihaly Csikszentmihalyi says a flow state is *"a state in which people are so involved in an activity that nothing else seems to matter; the experience is so enjoyable that people will continue to do it even at a great cost, for the sheer sake of doing it."*

He actually borrowed the term 'flow state' from a mountain climber because they need to be so present when hanging off the side of a cliff, there is no other option to ensure their safety.

"The purpose of flow is to keep on flowing," the climber told him. "Not looking for a peak or a utopia but staying in the flow ... there is no possible reason to climb except the climbing itself."

The shadow side of this is when we want to stay in this bubble of bliss and withdraw from the world and its responsibilities. It's a bit like trying to call a surfer onto land on a day when the waves are pumping. "Just one more," they will say. We'll avoid the 'real world' in order to ride the creative rush of inspiration and make it last as long as possible.

Some mystics stay in the cave in a meditative state and enlighten themselves on behalf of all humanity. Some humans use this flow state to avoid pain, also called spiritual bypassing. As with all altered states of consciousness, there is a shadow side to everything. The key is to break often. Not like glass, but like waves. This charm inside you is designed to break you open over and over again.

PRACTICE MEDITATION

Compass Meditation

Being disoriented for a while is a healthy part of transformation that reorganises our energy. We can spin round and round and feel lost, often looking outside of ourselves for someone else to tell us where to go. At the other end of the scale, we can become fixed and get our needle stuck on one way only because we can't let go of control.

Either way, you need a reliable compass to steer through rough waters and find the horizon again. One thing is always constant, and that's your True North. It never changes.

The following meditation will guide you back to True North.

1. *Find yourself a seat. Let yourself settle in, sitting on top of a cushion or with some back support. Bring your spine into a nice, straight position. As you feel safe, close your eyes, taking a nice, deep breath in through your nose, letting it out the mouth with a sigh. Can you sense your shoulders dropping? Inhale, breathe in. Exhale, open the mouth. Let's do that one more time. Inhale, open the mouth. Exhale to empty. Just let it all go, relaxing the back of the neck. Become aware of your body and where your body is sitting in space.*
   Bring your awareness to your skin and sense the spiritual skin that you're sitting in. How has it arrived in this moment? Imagine you can breathe through your skin, sensing that it's porous, sensing that aliveness, or even a buzzing sensation on different parts of your skin. Notice where it might be stronger or more subtle.
   Imagine now that you're sitting on your favourite beach in nature in the middle of summer. See where you locate yourself. Imagine that you're sitting on either a comfortable beach chair or a colourful beach towel, or perhaps you're just sitting directly on the sand. You're facing the ocean. As you sit here, you sense there's a gentle breeze coming off the water. You can hear the waves. There's nobody around you. It's just you

sitting on this beach, with maybe the sound of a faint seagull. You feel very relaxed. There is nowhere else to go. Sense a homecoming, a feeling that you may have been to this beach before.

2. *Now bring your attention to the centre of your heart, focusing all your awareness on your heart space. Imagine that your heart is like the face of a compass. See a round compass being placed over or within your heart. It has four directions, clearly marked north, south, east, and west. Take your next breath into the centre of your compass. Exhale to soften.*

3. *Bring your awareness to the east side of your compass. East is where the sun rises at dawn, and it represents new beginnings. It's where you look to receive inspiration, motivation and light. When you look towards the east of your heart, ask yourself, what is it that you're ready to start? What are you curious to start in your life? What are you feeling motivated to begin? What inspires you? Notice what is revealed to you.*

4. *Bring your awareness to the west side of the compass in your heart. West is the direction where the sun sets. It's where we move towards rest. Notice what the west is asking you. What is it that you need to rest or replenish in your life? What is asking for rest and reinvention? Perhaps it's an old pattern, or a part of your physical body that needs rest, like your nervous system, or it could be your mind, your mental health, or your spirit. Does your spirit need a break? Notice what the west shows you.*

5. *Now bring your awareness to the south. The direction of south points down towards the Earth. Straightway, you can sense gravity pulling towards the Earth. What in your life is ready*

to die? What do you need to let go of for good? You might even imagine that you are looking at the dirt where a hole is dug in the ground and a headstone, a blank headstone. As you look at the headstone, what word appears on it? What in your life is ready to be buried? This is a natural part of death and birth and rebirth. What cycle has ended or is ready to end? Notice what the headstone reveals to you. Feel ok with that.

6. *Now turn your attention towards the north, the direction that points and shoots straight up towards the stars. Imagine it like a laser beam, or a light moving up through your throat, through the crown of your head and into the vast sky. North represents your truth. Intuition. What is the question you ask your intuition?*

   What is it that you're guiding me towards?
   What is my truth?

   Where am I being pulled towards, that is serving my expansion and my growth?
   What is it that my charming creature wants for me? And if this charm had a voice, what would she say to me?

   If everything dies and changes, then what is really true?
   If everything is impermanent, what part of me remains?

   What is my truth?

7. *Take a deep breath in through the nose. Let it out through the mouth. Allow yourself to be excited by this dream. Allow yourself to dream even bigger. Your true north is guided by your compass. This direction is your soul. You can't go wrong. Whenever you feel disorientated or confused or stuck, come back to this thing, this one thing that stays the same about you,*

for it is your essence. Now imagine that you're looking directly out towards the horizon of your ocean, your eyes penetrating the infinite line ahead of you. See that horizon as the part of you that is constant, that doesn't change. It's always there and is unlimited.

Take a deep breath. Let it out, placing both hands over your heart. Offer yourself some care and compassion. Feel the Goddess or the God of nature surrounding you, supporting you, excited for what lies ahead. When you're ready, you can gently start to lower your hands and open your eyes.

Pick up your pen and your journal. Draw a circle with the four directions. Fill up one page, and write the feedback, the information shown to you, putting a few words at the end of each of the four directions, maybe even drawing a picture or a symbol.

JOURNAL PROMPTS

1. List at least three situations in which you ignored your intuition.
2. How did you know that you were no longer connected to your intuition?
3. Remember a time when you acted on your intuition during a crisis, difficult decision, or challenge. Write down all that you can recall.
4. How do you know that the information came from your own intuition?
5. Take a moment to consider the three types of intuition presented here.
   Reflect on when you have encountered them in the form of Survival, Deep Communion, or Flow State?
   Write down all that you can remember about these experiences.

CHAPTER 6

STORIES OF A WHITE PRIVILEGED WOMAN

*"People travel to wonder
at the height of the mountains,
at the huge waves of the seas,
at the long course of the rivers,
at the vast compass of the ocean,
at the circular motion of the stars,
and yet they pass by themselves
without wondering."*
—Saint Augustine

I'm twenty-one years old and I decide to move from Brisbane to Melbourne. The voice of 'Bris Vegas' booms in my ears, "Get outta here, kid. This aint your place." I have five dollars and fifty cents in my pocket to see me through until next week. Arriving in a new state as an unemployed university graduate has its advantages, though. Ok, there's an underlying panic of uncertainty, but for the first time, I sense the freedom of adult possibility. My relationship with home consumed by this insistent drive to travel away from it.

My intuition is guiding me towards this rite of passage. It's scary but staying at home indefinitely is more frightening. I'm physically an adult and yet I'm a small fish in a much bigger pond now, a creature surrounded by diversity. This new environment is peppered with lessons yet to be learned.

Perhaps I am seeking what some other cultures around the world are so good at: marking the transition from adolescence to adulthood. I'm ready for some kind of ritual that celebrates this urgency to give purpose to my life. I don't even know where to begin. I've landed in the bayside suburb of St Kilda in the middle of winter. It is not yet programmed into me that a long warm coat, boots and a beanie are part of the uniform. My teeth chatter as the freezing ocean breeze whips across my body. I walk down the street, passing a Middle Eastern man, an Indian woman, European backpackers and Asian mothers pushing strollers. People look different to me. The cultural melting pot of humans in this continental city fills my spirit with curiosity. I can hear a variety of accents talking quickly, laughing and socialising at the plentiful bars lining the street. A trio of three young Caucasian guys cruise confidently in my direction, boldly checking me out. My breath shivers as it tries to find a warm response. Awkwardly, I smile back.

I can smell the sea mixed with cuisines from all around the world. I can see a rainbow of colours. Skin, hair and eyes come in many palettes, each person with a story and a background they've travelled from. It's the year 2000, and we're entering a new millennium. This portal is a promising invitation to burst forwards into a new age. I'm still too young to know what that means and too old to not say yes. All I know is that staying in a smaller city feels suffocating because of all that repetition with the same familiar crowds. It's time for the unknown and creating space for growth and new relationships, for drifting down a tunnel with new dreams, desires and ambitions. Turning a bustling corner, I walk towards the supermarket to buy whatever I can with my loose change for dinner. Mmm, maybe cheese and crackers. Or an apple. Or two-minute noodles. I don't know what I'll be able to get. I don't look behind me as I cut through the dark underground carpark, or to my left or to my right. Blind to the pedestal I have placed myself on, I feel like I know everything already about my new neighbourhood and the entitled space I take up.

As I approach the back entry to Woolworths, I notice four people seated outside, all of them looking my way. They are wearing similar clothes, slogan t-shirts and tracksuit pants, and the concrete area they occupy is surrounded with empty bottles and rubbish. I keep walking and avoid eye contact.

An Aboriginal woman within the group yells for my attention.

"Hey, you! Do you have ten cents?"

I pretend not to hear and continue walking.

"Hey, I'm talking to you. Do you have ten cents?" she asks again.

I look down silently. My hands are in my pockets, and I grip tightly onto the only cash I have left. My palms are sweaty and sticky. Ahead of me, I spot the shop doors sliding open and I dash forwards, seeking safety on the other side. Instinctively, I know I'm being followed into the store. My energy field is alive with another presence. The hairs on the back of my neck stand up, telling me to pay attention. Be alert! As my breath becomes caught in my upper chest, I turn around. I come face to face with the woman, who, to my surprise, is double my size when upright, and now one metre away from me.

She lunges forwards and stands on top of each of my feet so I can't move.

"Aghhhhhh," is the noise I make as pain shoots through.

I'm stuck to the shiny supermarket floor next to the fresh produce section under fluorescent lights. Adrenalin surges up my spine but it's impossible to flee. Why can't I run? It's a simple survival response my brain cannot compute.

Her full bodyweight pushes down on each bone, my toes crushed under a pair of dirty Nike sneakers.

I want to look away, call for help. Can't someone see what's happening?

She presses her nose against my nose. We stare at each other, eyeball to eyeball. There's no air to breathe between us, only the sweet sharp fumes of ethanol that waft up my nose.

"I asked you for ten cents!" she shouts as chunks of her spit rebound off my forehead and nose.

I keep holding my breath. That time at band camp. Being spat on.

Girls pointing. My inner invisible wounded child is right beside me. Tears begin to spill down my cheeks.

Help! Why isn't someone helping? The thoughts spin around in my head. I'm completely frozen and fixed on her pupils. There is fear in her eyes. Time stands still as a rush of energy whooshes through us both simultaneously. For a fraction of a nanosecond, my soul comes online and a flash of recognition passes through me.

"Thwack."

Her right fist lands on one of my kidneys and I bend over, clutching my lower back.

"Ughhh."

This sound is forced out of my lower lungs as I pause and stay hunched, waiting for another blow.

Nothing happens. I raise my head and look up. I don't know where she's gone.

Everyone in the supermarket is moving in slow motion as I slowly stand. Besides a bruise, I'm not physically hurt, but my body has shut down and gone numb. Nobody in the supermarket comes to check if I'm ok. What the hell? It's as if everyone is wearing blinders or something. Or perhaps I'm playing dead and have turned invisible as some sort of superpower to survive.

Dazed and blurry, I stumble down aisle seven and grab a can of tomatoes and a packet of spaghetti and make my way to the checkout. I hand over the money without saying a word. For a brief moment, I stood in someone else's shoes. I experienced everything at once. Shock. Shame. Loneliness. Terror. Confusion. Powerless.

I wonder where the woman is now. Maybe she didn't really want ten cents. Most likely, she wanted to be seen, heard and respected. Like we all do. I swallow the dryness and walk down the road to my new home.

Exercising your power of choice means you need to heal the traumas from your past. It means owning your stories. That means owning the scared you, the recovering you, the unforgiving you, the unhealed you, and all the secrets the ashamed you has thrived in.

I had an ongoing sick feeling in the pit of my stomach before I wrote this part of my story which is my intuition's way of telling me it's time to write about this part! I've never expressed this story publicly, but owning up to it means if it heals me, it will help heal someone else.

When I was at school, I was told I could have it all. Not only could I have it, I was it!

White. Straight. Thin. Able-bodied. Educated. Middle class. I belonged, and every system supported my belonging.

My whiteness meant I wasn't suspected of shoplifting when I stole a sports bra in year eight. My whiteness meant I wore a uniform of designer labels to fit in with all the other private school clones. My whiteness meant I was picked for a gymnastics team because pale skin was the preferred shade to match the rest of the group. The one Asian girl was given her special 'solo' part again. God forbid we looked different from each other! That would not be perfect and would put the judges right off. After the incident in the supermarket with the Aboriginal woman, I realised my unearned privilege and unconscious biases had cost her a basic human right—to be respected and treated as an equal. And I needed to understand how little I actually knew about trauma.

We all need to take responsibility when we hurt each other. Whether you're throwing punches, hiding knives in your words or being complicit in your silence, it's not ok. What we walk past will continue.

A racist system that is broken makes people sick. People like me. People like all of us numbly walking past. To walk past another human being in desperate need is dehumanising. So why do we do it? Our patriarchal oppressive society has enabled violence since the day of colonisation. It's a system that prioritises control over charm. Trauma rises to be healed at different stages of our growth. Suppressing it feeds our unconscious biases and keeps us all in a collective dysregulated nervous system.

Tracey Michael Lewis-Giggetts writes on how the reality of systemic oppression affects a black woman's ability to be safely vulnerable, *"We can believe in our inherent worth and value all we want, but moving through the world where our very survival often depends on an acceptance of dehumanization makes healing from trauma complicated. We are swimming in a cesspool of shame, breathing in our own contempt—to the extent that many of us believe that the only way to truly live is to grow steely-hearted gills and adapt."*

I know I still have blind spots about what people who are different to me endure on a daily basis. I cannot keep looking away like I did outside the supermarket that day. It's with a pounding pulse and shaky hands that I publish this story because I also know I'll probably read it in a couple of years and see racism in it I can't see today. I'll do it anyway.

Dr Maya Angelou writes, *"Do the best you can until you know better. Then when you know better, do better."*

During 2023, I was part of a six-month coaching group called the Power Collective with facilitator Kemi Nekvapil. Equality was one of the guiding principles of the P.O.W.E.R. acronym that we studied. Kemi is an all-round wonderful human and I unapologetically will continue to be a devotee and hang on all her words of wisdom. Kemi is one of Australia's leading coaches and a highly sought-after international speaker. Her book, *"Power",* had a big impact on me. So much so that I also sought one-to-one coaching to help me navigate through a challenging year of becoming.

Kemi writes, *"When we don't own everything that has happened to us, what others have done to us, what we have done to others and what we have done to ourselves, we end up hustling for our worth or living somebody else's life because we no longer know who we are."*

During our work together, I was prompted to look deep into the areas of my life I didn't feel powerful. On the topic of allyship, I reflected hard on what I'd experienced to date working with marginalised individuals and groups. In her book, *"Me and White Supremacy"*, Layla Saad writes, *"The first thing to understand is that allyship is not an identity but a practice. A person with white privilege does not get to proclaim themselves as an ally to BIPOC but rather seeks to practice allyship consistently."*

I knew I needed clear counsel on the complexity as I responded to this coaching question.

Am I ready to be an ally?

I've been in the arena for three years, learning, unlearning and falling flat on my face. I've been doing the cultural awareness courses, the white privilege work, partnering with black-owned businesses, reading black-authored books, going to music concerts and cultural performances, travelling to different lands and absorbing what the Traditional Owners have to say, listening to ancient stories, hiking on Country and connecting with the ancestors, educating my kids and British monarchist in-laws, decolonising my scheduled and conditioned mind, investing hours of time in conversation, promoting black businesses, offering my classes to black teachers and more. I voluntarily immersed my whole soul into it.

My fingernails dirty, hair sweaty, back hurting, I made sure my body felt punished and felt the pain inflicted on every slave that's ever been chained. Walking on Aboriginal land, in the desert, leading retreats, I decided I was responsible for the deaths, the shame, the history and the stolen children. I needed to absorb the guilt and sorrow so nobody else had to feel it anymore.

I tried to walk in a black person's shoes before I could even walk in my own. I wanted to own their stories like they were mine. I gave my power away when what they wanted was for me to be able to stand in my power. They didn't need my power. They needed to see their own power reflected back to them. They didn't need me to save them. They needed to see me save myself.

I've breathed in the white man's game, expectations and air thick with comparison, performance, striving and proving. I've tried to show on the outside what doesn't yet exist on the inside, while unlearning such deep conditioning.

I'm not ready to be an ally, because healing relationships demand equal powerful partners.
I'm working on brave.

Kemi replied, "I was deeply moved when I read this, Tina, and there is only one question I want to ask you: 'I'm not ready to be an ally' seems binary. It is as if you believe you are one or the other. Ally or racist? In my experience, everything you have written here is proof that you are an ally. Why would you do the work if you weren't? What sits in the middle? What can you allow yourself to be while also not being there yet? And to be honest, what does 'being there' even look like?"

I took a pause to consider everything and work through a shame spiral during my vulnerability hangover. As a product of a corrupt system stacked in my favour, I know the solution to inequality is not to wallow in self-loathing or centre my own painful feelings. My discomfort stems from being pinned with an identity that labels me, inescapably, as an oppressor. That activates the wounded Attached Inner Child who wants to be a 'good girl' and keep everyone happy. This is 'the work' for white privileged women everywhere. Justice will never fulfill its destiny unless those with power confront their privilege and grow into spiritual maturity. We're not going to empower others by disempowering ourselves and staying small and silent.

Own it first. Face the fear. Do the work.

I'm inspired by Bell Hook's quote, *"Privilege is not in and of itself bad; what matters is what we do with privilege. We have to share our resources and take direction about how to use our privilege in ways that empower those who lack it."*

As I took a deep breath in and a big sigh out, I replied to Kemi.

I've had some time to think since writing this and realised that allyship is very similar to the spiritual path. Once you get on, you can't get off. Maybe if I view it as a path, it can't be binary, just windy and full of twists and turns. Curious for what's around the corner. Once we heal our own traumas, we can transform our wounds into wisdom and be of service to others.

That was nine Tinas ago. Saying this with a smile is important, as is having affection and love for our earlier versions, when we were recovering from something, learning, growing and figuring stuff out. Boy, do I have more stories to tell. That Tina was scared but she's accepting that being in the middle of anything is messy.

I'm nine years old and running barefoot around my backyard collecting lizards from the garden. I've made them a temporary home in a shoebox filled with leaves and rocks. There are three—then seven—then ten tiny reptiles all freaking out in a cardboard cube.

My inquisitiveness peaked at studying little creatures to see how they interact and play furiously. The bigger ones are still and less interested in my obstacle course. They don't care to be tamed or told how to behave as their offspring scurry and hurry, doing circle work around the perimeter.

Ring, ring, ring.

I hear the phone go off in the downstairs living area. I am the closest to the house as Mum and Dad are gardening outside so I bolt inside to pick it up.

I answer the phone, "Hello, this is ..."

A woman on the other end interjects.

"Hello there. You don't know me. We've never met before. Isn't that sad? I'm your grandmother."

I can't recall clearly what happened after that. The phone was grabbed by my mother and there were stern words spoken and not much else explained. I grew up not knowing my family on my father's side. A decision was made on my behalf to protect me from abusive relatives and strained relationships. I accepted this and trusted my parents' choice—they only wanted love and safety for us.

It's a common story that families become fractured, displaced, broken and bleeding for various reasons. My father's parents and grandparents came from Russia and fled from conflict revolutions by immigrating to Australia over the last one hundred years.

I have generational ghosts living inside me and taking up residence in my cells. Memories and habits that aren't mine have been woven into the fabric of my DNA. Intuitively, our bodies keep the score. It's no secret that scientifically our issues in our tissues come to surface at some stage on this spiritual path.

Traumas and wars that are not my fault are my responsibility to heal, passed on for hundreds of years by bodies across cultures in clumps like entangled tumbleweeds. I'm a survivor of other people's pain. I'm an expression of my ancestors' joy and storytelling gifts. And I'm creating the conditions for future legacies yet to be born.

During one of Melbourne's lockdowns, I decide to investigate my family further. Fuelled by boredom and blessed with time, I order an Ancestry 'spit in a plastic tube' test to explore my DNA results. I've always felt like a complete mystery to myself, made up of many versions with indigenous roots to unknown lands.

The package arrives in the post, and I unwrap it eagerly to reveal its contents. Following the instructions, step by step, I set it up on the kitchen bench to begin the process.

Sluuuuurp, pfffft, I snort and make a throaty sound.

A big dollop of spit drips from my mouth as I watch it in slow motion fall from my lips, aiming for the target below. All the secrets in the saliva, my thoughts marvel. I consciously take in a bigger sip of air and notice my heartbeat quicken as a memory surfaces. Lying on the bottom bunk bed, a drop of spit lands in my eye, girls snickering. I'm alone in a crowded room again.

Exhaling forcefully, I sense eleven-year-old little Tina standing right beside me. Watching the saliva slide to the bottom of the clear test tube, a lifetime of stories and shame is contained in a tiny vial of liquid. This blueprint of the past is ready to be analysed and summarised in a neat report.

A month later and I receive an email from Ancestry saying, *"Your DNA results are in!"*

The information comes casually, as a breakdown of statistics:
- Eastern Europe and Russia – 46%
- England and North-western Europe – 31%
- Ireland – 10%
- Sweden and Denmark – 7%
- Scotland – 5%
- Mongolia and Central Asia – 1%

A pie chart confirms that I'm a global pizza made up of many flavours!

If everyone ran this experiment and reduced our lives to fractions, we could assume we'd mostly be a combination of many cultural origins across the planet. From the roof of a wood-fired oven, our pizzas would look similar; colourful spinning wheels filled with diverse toppings. But from the base, at a granular level, the reality is very different for each pizza. Some carry much heavier toppings and bear the weight of a bigger load to support.

Dr Gabor Mate writes, "It's all too easy for the privileged among us to assume we walk the same streets as everyone else. Though a satellite view of Earth may suggest we do, that's not how it plays out at ground level."

At street level, you come face to face with reality that the beast of inequality means not all charming creatures are given the same chance in life.

So, how can we break the cycles of intergenerational trauma and quicken the collective healing needed right now?

We can begin by transforming the influences of past wounds and atrocities on ourselves, our families and our ancestral bloodlines. This starts with learning the truth and unlearning the lies we've been told or shielded from. We must become better navigators for the charm that wants to bring forth clarity, wisdom, and dreams.

All transformation, and collective healing, needs to start with the self. We begin with our own burdens and do the work. This doesn't mean we can't help others at the same time we're healing our past. If anything, it supports our evolution.

As James Baldwin writes, *"Not everything that is faced can be changed; but nothing can be changed until it is faced."*

JOURNAL PROMPTS

Reflect on the following when considering owning your stories of privilege.

1. Are you in this for the long haul?
2. Do you realise that deconstructing unconscious conditioning is shadow work?
3. Are you prepared for the reassessment of values that comes with walking a path of allyship?
4. Are you driven by the need for recognition and achievement, or can you work at the pace of trust?
5. Do you have daily devotional practices that support this embodiment process?
6. Are you drawn to explore your own ancestral and generational healing?

Part II

The following chapters include seven guiding sign posts you can put into practise immediately while travelling your Intuitive Mountain Map.

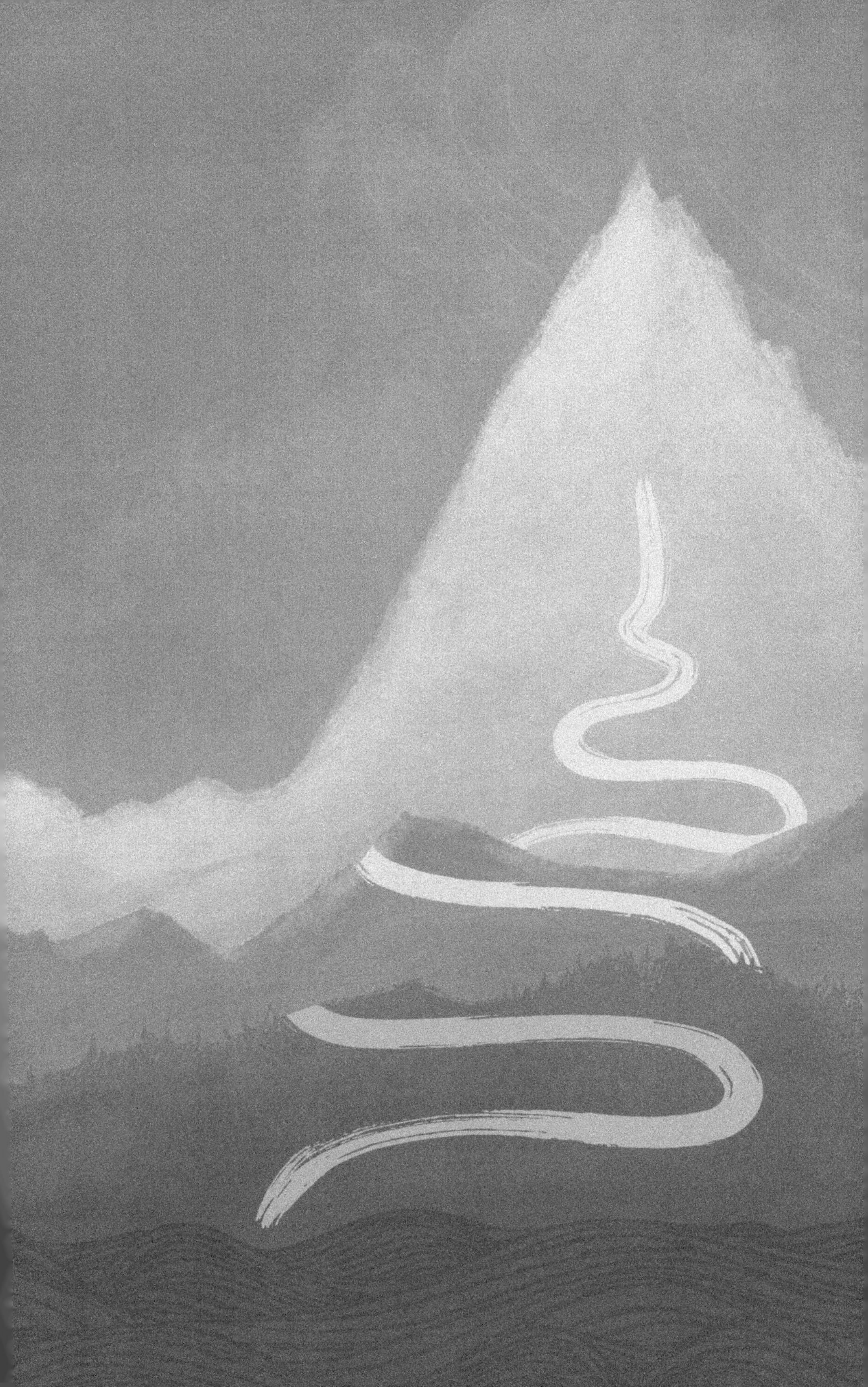

Ganesha

CHAPTER 7

MIDLIFE MOUNTAIN

Chakra: Base [Muladhara]
Consciousness: Deep Sleep
Mantra: Om Gam Ganapatiyei Namaha
Location: Base of spine/cox, legs, feet, immune system, adrenal glands
Element: Earth
Challenge: Fear of not belonging, fear of being unsafe
Power: Grounding, safety, protection, security
Breath: Ujayi Pranayama/Sighing Breath

"All know the way, but few actually walk it."
—Buddha

My nervous system shifts into overdrive, so I call my sister.

"I'm on the way to the hospital," my voice trembles.

"Why?" Peta asks.

My anxiety spills into the receiver.

"Because my GP told me to. I think I'm having an allergic reaction to the COVID vaccine."

"Ok. It's going to be ok," she reassures me. "Take some deep breaths. Call me when you get there."

My hands grip tighter onto the steering wheel while holding my breath at the traffic lights. Tilting the rear view mirror to take a glimpse at my neck, the sight of the rash crawling up towards my chin causes a memory to flash.

Nervous.

Humiliated.

If fear had a face, it is definitely the colour red. I stay focused while driving underground into the hospital carpark. As I enter through the sliding doors, the smell of sterility through my double facemasks instantly triggers another traumatic memory I've buried but can never be fully extinguished. I sit in the emergency department waiting room, waiting for my emergency to be important enough to jump the queue, trying not to scratch the itchy redness that has wrapped itself around my neck. The decision on whether to get the Pfizer vaccine or not is still strangling me.

I get ushered to a cubicle and told to wait some more.

The patient next door yells at the staff, "Can someone see me! Helloooo? I've been here for two hours!"

It's clear that being in a hospital in the middle of a global pandemic is not a calming place for the nerves.

Finally, a doctor walks in and asks if I have chest pain.

"No, but I have this lumpy red rash spreading down to my chest and my breathing is a bit wheezy and I've got a cracking headache," I reply.

The doctor pauses for all of three seconds. Then, without examining me, he says, "I'm just going to check with the head of the department because he is an expert on this. I'll be back."

It doesn't make me feel any better that he needs reassurance. Then I remember that I'm in the biggest public emergency hospital in the state—he may be a student doctor.

He returns with a bounce in a step and the confidence of a young colt.

"Your symptoms are not a serious side effect. I'll order you some antihistamines and you can be discharged."

Apparently, I wasn't dead enough, so I walk through the hospital searching for some comfort, something to relieve my pain. I head over to the vending machine and prescribe myself a can of Coca-Cola. It's another vessel filled with 'unknown' chemical ingredients I'm willing to pour into me. The ol' black medicine. I'm hoping it kills every bug it comes into contact with on my insides. Instant gratification!

Back home, and a few days later, my symptoms subside, leaving me with a foul taste in my mouth and a deep gratitude for the intelligence of my body. How does it know how to heal? And what is it trying to tell me? This eruption through my skin was talking to me. I promised my body I would listen better and pause before injecting or putting anything into it. I decide to take my body for a walk to give it some fresh air as Banjo waits eagerly, panting at the front door. One of my neighbours I often see in the street is an eccentric lady whose mop of blond curly hair matches her two shih tzus. Our dogs stop to chat and sniff. I've always enjoyed a quick chat with her, mostly about the fitness industry, as she's an instructor and works at the local gym.

"Morning. Are you still teaching?" she asks.

"Just on Zoom, like everyone else," I reply.

"Will you sign my petition? I'm one of the 'crazy' ones, you know, an anti-vaxxer. I'm campaigning to save the fitness industry from the mandatory laws on vaccines," she states enthusiastically.

I listen patiently, mostly because I can't get a word in edgewise. Just be patient and be present to what she's saying, I tell myself. After what seems like forever, I yank on Banjo's lead, signalling my need to find that fresh air without so many words congesting the atmosphere.

"You can join my Facebook group," she says. "I now have over five-hundred members, and we are going to march in protest next weekend.

It's a great way to meet people and we chat all the time online."

"Thanks." I try to make my getaway, but she keeps talking.

"I'm also selling all my possessions on Facebook marketplace. I can't wait to sell my house and get out of these lockdowns. China is about to take over, and I need to get as far away from the 5G vibes as possible. I'm going to grow my own vegetables. I've learned how to do it on Facebook!"

She was just getting warmed up on how Facebook will solve the world's problems. I think it's incredible we have these online technology platforms to communicate with each other. I also think they have the potential to cause a lot of harm, which is the reason why I closed my Facebook account. Too many dysregulated nervous systems were trying to get their Metta point across.

Those thoughts happen inside my head. I smile and say, "C'mon, Banjo, we've got to go."

I book in to see my GP to prepare for round two of a booster shot. My nervous system wants to flee, mostly because it has already learned the first time that it could be a slippery slide down the stairs again to the emergency department.

My GP says, "Don't worry. I've spoken to an allergy expert, and we have a plan. Take these steroids and antihistamines and Nurofen and Panadol before you get the jab, and you'll be good to go."

I try to comprehend in my non-expert mind all the extra chemicals I need to consume, on top of the vial of vaccine, to protect me from a virus which I have 0.001 per cent chance of falling seriously ill with.

I pause to listen to my body and what it is saying. My head is louder. It is thinking that the only way I'm going to be able to fly to the Northern Territory and lead this retreat is if I'm double vaxxed according to government border rules.

My heartbeat races and my palms get sweaty. I need to psych myself up for this next round. I need a coach or a pep talk to get me into shape so I can walk through the door.

I turn on the Tony Robbins podcast as I drive to the vaccination clinic for my appointment.

"If you get in your head, you're dead," he yells in his gruff, unmistakable voice.

I repeat this mantra over and over.

"If I get in my head, I'm dead. If I get in my head, I'm dead."

Once there, drawing on some serious courage, I take my place in the line and roll up my sleeve.

"Next!" a voice yells.

"Name? Date of birth? Address?" she demands.

I get ushered into a sheep cubicle and told to wait. The nurse comes in with her plastic tray of needles. My stomach is churning with anxiety, and I cling onto my handbag holding the icy cold can of Coke, ready to wash it down while I'm in the fifteen-minute post holding bay.

"Are you nervous?" she intuitively asks.

"Yesss, I had a reaction to the first jab, and I hope it doesn't happen again."

She stops what she's doing and looks at me.

"Oh, didn't you get a medical exemption?" Then she whispers, "You know you don't have to do this. I have heaps of nursing friends who are refusing to get vaccinated. You can walk out of here and think about it. It might cause another more serious adverse effect. I'm not sure I should give you this."

This is unexpected counsel coming from a health professional who is gripping a needle four inches away from my arm. My heart is pounding in my chest as my breath becomes fast and shallow. I look at her intently and say, "Give me the vaccine. I'm ready."

When she doesn't do anything, I say, "I'm not leaving here until you jab me."

At this point, I am so psyched up that I've made my decision and I'm not going to let anyone come between me and the rest of my travelling life. She inserts the needle and I respond, "Thank you" with a shaky voice, before getting up from my chair and walking with wobbly knees out the door.

Both humans and animals have a built-in protection mechanism which is our survival intuition. My dog is five years old and can't walk downstairs. He freezes at the top and starts shaking like a leaf. He is a charming creature, yet he has an animal instinct that paralyses him based on a traumatic experience he had as a puppy when he slid down the staircase. The job of our nervous system is to keep us safe. Unfortunately, if our mind is stuck in a survival loop of imagined threats, our body does not know the difference and will react appropriately. It is our animal nature to hold on to past traumas to warn us and keep us safe from repeating the same thing. What I've experienced from living in a body stuck in survival mode is that fear gives really bad advice. Terrible advice. It is the one thing that sabotages our empowerment journey and blocks us from acting on our intuition. Many people are more likely to sabotage their transformation than to enthusiastically participate in their personal healing. For this reason, we begin by regulating our nervous system so we can tell the difference between the fearful shadow saboteur voice and the voice of truth.

Intuition lives in your body. Anxious sensations of tightness, pain, breathlessness and contraction are our intuition communicating with us when it wants our attention. All of these bodily cues are our inner self talking to us. When we're dysregulated, it feels like terror to make any kind of decision. We are caught in an anxious loop, and it can be so hard to get out of the fear.

> These fears live in our subconscious energy centres, or the seven chakras, and include:
> 1. The fear of being unsafe
> 2. The fear of losing control
> 3. The fear we're not enough
> 4. The fear of rejection
> 5. The fear of authentic expression
> 6. The fear of seeing the truth
> 7. The fear of death

We are going to walk through every one of these fears together. We are on a pilgrimage and the Intuitive Mountain we're exploring is *you*.

Navigating your Intuitive Mountain Map

When I began writing, I was nervous because I was in the middle of a process of re-discovering who I was again. Unsure, uncertain and losing confidence, I was in the process of walking through the 'midlife mountain' which is me. In the next chapters, I share the map I created, which includes specifically designed practices that support you to release unhelpful patterns in the body and mind and carve a new path for possibility and spirit to flow. As the path towards your intuition compels you to make sense of who you are and what you want, you grow a relationship with the person inside your own skin. It won't make you more understandable to others, but it does force you into a direct experience with your own unedited charm.

The realisation that I am in charge of my life has continued to surface through every chapter. Few truths are as profound as discovering how powerful every one of my choices are, even the silent, small choices we make for ourselves on a day-to-day basis. We have the power to shift the quality of our lives with the very next choice. When we're confused or afraid to make that choice, then it is an invitation to turn towards your 'mountain'.

Historically, mountains have been used as metaphors for the Hero's Journey, spiritual awakenings and transcendent experiences that guide us towards our highest potential. For this purpose, we are not going to ascend to the top of the mountain, we are going into the very centre of it. At its core, you'll discover that you are the Intuitive Mountain. This is where True North lives—your most authentic expression.

This is an excerpt from *"When Things Fall Apart"* by Buddhist nun, Pema Chodron. *"Spiritual awakening is frequently described as a journey to the top of a mountain. In the process of discovering Bodhichitta [the awakened heart], the journey goes down, not up. It's as if the mountain pointed toward the centre of the earth instead of reaching into the sky. Instead of transcending the suffering of all creatures, we move toward the turbulence and doubt. We explore the reality and unpredictability of insecurity and pain, and we try not to push it away. If it takes years, if it takes lifetimes, we let it be as it is.*

At our own pace, without speed or aggression, we move down and down and down. With us, move millions of others, our companions in awakening from fear. At the bottom, we discover water, the healing water of Bodhichitta. Right down there in the thick of things, we discover the love that will not die."

Our intuition knows what our mountain is. Perhaps it is a fear of losing control, fear of failing, fear of rejection or fear of not knowing who we are or what our purpose is. This unstable foundation invites us to begin at the bottom. Science shows us that like a pyramid, when we widen and strengthen the base, there is more space in the middle to hold extra heat or life-force energy. Our ability then to grow is capable of expanding deeper into its centre.

It's often an unconscious part of us that is holding us back from what we want, and in truth, it is almost always a result of an accumulation of little traumas, conditioning and childhood maladaptive coping mechanisms, all of which are increasing the pressure inside the mountain. Those charming children have carried us this far, but now need something to change inside in order to carry us further. In the same way a volcano implodes, release ourself into the fire so we can create the life we are trying to lead. Each chapter moving forwards, we'll traverse through and explore a different layer of our seven energy centres, or Hindu Chakras in the Yogic Tradition, that direct us through our Intuitive Mountain Map. Think of them as signposts on the trail to transformation.

Like many hero's journeys, this includes:
- The challenges and fears you'll face
- The power you'll unearth
- The goddesses and deities that support your evolution

Each goddess/deity relates to a particular part of our charming creature and has a signature energy which we invoke when chanting the mantras and feeling into their spirit. We can muse on how they influence our consciousness, but when we do the energy practices, we have a direct experience with their power.

In Hinduism, many goddesses have a charming creature called a vahana (Sanskrit: 'mount' or 'vehicle'). The creature that serves as the vehicle supports them in their work and transports them across multiple dimensions all over the universe. The vahana is their chariot or means to move forwards.

Durga is depicted astride a lion or a tiger, Saraswati a swan. Medusa is supported by snakes, and we have already met Ganesha and his mouse. In essence, the vehicle is different, but the path is the same. We are all on the journey to liberation and transformation. Snakes are represented across cultures, and in Greek mythology, serpents are considered symbols for transformation: messengers between the upper and lower worlds. Archetypally a sign of death and rebirth, the snake that does not shed its skin will surely die.

Our lives are continually influenced by archetypal patterns and their subtle magnetic influences that shape our psyches. Their powers can untangle years of karmic knots and cleanse our mental and emotional bodies of fears to radically change our perception. They all exist inside of us already and have been worshipped for thousands of years because the archetypal stories are timeless. Allow each deity to become a refuge, like a dear friend that offers comfort and a sense of home. By walking humbly through our inner midlife mountain, we'll learn to see ourselves in each and every one of them. Altitude of spirit is the goal!

The Intuitive Mountain that stands at your feet is the calling and the doorway inwards.

Follow this map forwards. It's time for rebirth and renewal.

"Each breath we take contains hundreds of thousands of the inert, pervasive argon atoms that were actually breathed in his lifetime by the Buddha, and indeed contain parts of the 'snorts, sighs, bellows, shrieks' of all creatures that ever existed, or will ever exist."
—Peter Matthiessen

"Breath is a rhythm, and we breathe in and out thousands of times a day. Breathing involves an intimate relationship between our bodies and the ocean of air within which we suspire. A dozen senses inform us of rhythm, texture and qualities in each breath. Life is always inviting us into a deeper relationship with breath, with the pulsing of our hearts and emotions."
—Lorin Roche, "The Radiance Sutras"

PRACTICE BREATHWORK

Can your breath serve a bigger purpose than just keeping you alive?

Yes. Stop what you're doing and take three conscious breaths. Notice how you feel when you are aware of every inhale? You become present with life and suddenly open to a little bit of charm.

Cultural messaging may tempt you to believe that breathwork practice is for really spiritual people. It feels a bit out of reach for regular folk not walking through the rare air of the Himalayas or embarking on a forty-day pilgrimage through the desert. And while it is true that your modern life may resemble nothing like a travelling wanderer or twisted pretzel yogi, the inner journey—the Intuitive Mountain Map—is exactly the same for all of us. We're all spiritful seekers on a destined path, just longing to breathe a bit more peacefully in our own skin. Modern science has now made mainstream what yogis have known all along. Breathwork can help people overcome PTSD, anxiety, depression, autoimmune conditions, burnout and lifelong conditioning and generational trauma. It hosts a plethora of physical benefits.

And there's more.

Breathwork enhances your intuition. Intuition needs a certain landscape within your body in order for your fight/flight/freeze sympathetic nervous system to return to balance. Starting with a practice of conscious breathing, rest, stillness, silence, and solitude are essential so that you can listen with your inner ear. Breathwork is not just to regulate the nervous system, but to follow its feelings and what it wants to authentically express.

In each chapter for the rest of this book, we work our way through a different breathwork practice that clears a particular fear.

Wait a second. I sense you are maybe already tensing up around the idea of this being 'work' and worrying and doubting how you're going to fit it into your already overstuffed schedule.

Let me preface everything by emphasising how much I love fear and anxiety. I worry about those who have no self-doubt or anxiety. People who are certain and overly confident leave no space for curiosity. How to hold the full mystery of *'How is my new spiritful life going to look?'* is always to endure its other half, which is equal mystery of the unknowable. It's healthy to fear. It's a natural reaction to moving closer to the truth of our charming creature. And, in the same way that our breathwork practice does not end when we step off the yoga mat or cushion, we are going to integrate all of this into daily moments. We will want to immerse into the healing energy of our breathwork all the time, not just during the one hour of formal practice.

Walking the dog:
    I inhale for the count of four ...
Driving to work:
    I exhale for the count of six ...
Time to shower:
    I hum my mantra for five minutes ...
Lying in bed at 3.00 am:
    I consciously connect with my breath ...
See? Your shoulders are dropping already.

As your guide, I don't know how to give you five 'hacks' to beat anxiety, but I'll teach you how to *be* with it. I'm even hesitant to describe myself as a Breathwork 'Master' because the breath *is* the true master. I need to surrender to its power and not get too bossy or sure of how things will work out. The moment we believe we're in control of the practice is the moment we meet a lot of frustration followed by a truckload of humility. The breath is the master at showing us our humanness. Peak spiritual experiences or altered states of consciousness are not the goal, but can be a result of us returning to our natural state of unconditional charm.

A spiritful perspective is one in which matter and spirit are understood to have never been separate. Matter and spirit do an energetic dance and create each other. Every time you inhale, you are repeating the pattern of delivering spirit into matter. And every time you exhale, you are repeating the pattern of returning spirit to the Earth. It's a continuous incarnation cycle.

Breathwork is more than a technique, it's an art. It's a communion with life itself. There's nothing to achieve and no level to get to in order to be considered an 'advanced' breather. Throughout this book, you'll see the overall intention of breathwork is to no longer have to 'work' at the breathing but to enjoy the charming dance with it.

So, where do we end and where does the breath begin?

With more practice, we begin to experience that there is no boundary—only a fluid, mystical membrane that is constantly shifting depending on the stories we tell ourselves.

Some of the breathwork practices I share in this book come from ancient cultural traditions. Some are based on evidence-based scientific physiology studies. Regardless of their origin, they all promote the release of stress and fear from the places your body keeps the score. And they all have a unique charm and intention to help you live your intuition more fully.

PRACTICE BREATHWORK

SIGHING BREATH

WHAT IS ITS CHARM?

"The most relaxed person in the room is always the most powerful." These were the words I heard author Elizabeth Gilbert speak at a live event once and they never left me. To live powerfully, I've become a fan of *the sigh*. This means stopping and breathing out a giant 'fuck it'. It is such great medicine that I do it regularly and my family always knows where I am in the house because every ten minutes, they hear a loud 'Ahhhhhhhhh'.

Sighing soothes the vagus nerve, otherwise known as the soul nerve, which wanders from the base of our skull, through the vocal cords, and down around our organs and gut. Slow breathing gently opens up the vagus network which creates the conditions for physiological safety. The sigh of relief creates a gap and also enables us to let go of something right there and then rather than react. Often after we do this, intuition lands and gives us the next instruction or inspiration. This can be as simple as asking, *'What do I need to let go of?'* *'Stop. Sigh. Slow down,'* is my mantra.

THE TYPE OF FEAR IT LOVES
Fear of feeling unsafe or ungrounded.

HOW DO I DO IT?
1. Sit or lie in a comfortable position.
2. Close your eyes and take a big breath in through your nose, filling belly and chest.
3. Hold it for one second at the top.
4. Open your mouth and let out an audible sigh as your shoulders drop.
5. Repeat three times.

JOURNAL PROMPTS

1. What behaviours cause me to be ungrounded?
2. What does safety and support look like for me?
3. What is the obstacle I'd like to offer up to Ganesha?

It is traditional to offer prayers to Ganesha before beginning any important task. This is believed to bring good fortune and remove any obstacles that may be in the way.

To ensure a smooth path towards the centre of my Intuitive Mountain, I offer up this fear.

Saraswati

CHAPTER 8

LET GO OF CONTROL

Chakra:	Sacral [Svadhistana]
Consciousness:	Dream State
Mantra:	Om Eim Saraswatiyei Namaha
Location:	Sacrum, pelvis, hips, large intestine, sexual glands, bladder
Element:	Water
Challenge:	Fear of losing control
Power:	Creativity, trust in the flow, healthy relationships
Breath:	Nadi Sodhana Pranayama

"Be a good steward of your gifts. Protect your time. Feed your inner life. Avoid too much noise. Read good books, have good sentences in your ears. Be by yourself as often as you can. Walk."

—Jane Kenyon

Walking along the beach, the ferocious ocean spray whips my face, along with the windy offshore gusts. My daughters run ahead, laughing at the way their hair is blowing forwards, framing their faces from behind. Pointing ahead, there are birds and a commotion of flapping squawking madness.

"Look, it's eating," Leila yells.

Arriving closer to the scene, the big bird is a striking black crow. It must have found a dead fish. Whichever country you travel in, a crow always shows up sooner or later. There will be no signs of life and then, all of a sudden, a crow on the side of the road, on a bin or at a beach. As we near the crow, we see another bird coming into focus. It's not uncommon to witness predator crows pecking at meat on the ground, and I don't think much of it until I realise the bird being attacked is still alive.

"It's moving!" Zoe cries.

The girls run forwards to shoo the crow away in an attempt to protect the defenceless creature. Its wing is bent and dragging along the sand. Broken and unable to fly, it has webbed feet and a curved beak.

"It looks like a baby albatross," Zoe says.

The three of us stand around the feeble bird and form a human fence to shield it from further danger. So shattered and bony, the bird visibly shakes with fear. It should already be dead, but its eyes tell another story. Gigantic and bulging, the bird looks at us with utter determination. Its feathers are stuck together and caked with sand and crumbed shells. Meanwhile, the crow is not going anywhere. Perched just five metres away, its stark yellow eyes burn like laser beams at its prey.

"Don't fuck with my lunch," the crow communicates silently with all its puffed-up plumage.

We freeze in our stance, feet sinking further into the wet sand. I hope the crow will get bored and take flight, but it just stays there, staring at us. Staring at its lunch. Then staring back at us. I look at my watch. 11.00 am. Shit, we only have an hour until I have to check out of the Airbnb holiday house.

"C'mon, girls, we need to get back," I say assertively, except my body won't move.

"Mum, if we walk away, this sea bird will be eaten alive," Leila says.

I need to make a choice but am paralysed. I reach for my phone but remember I left it back at the house. Can't phone a friend for advice now.

An older couple walk towards us, seemingly on their morning stroll. Great, maybe they have a mobile and we can call the wildlife rescue team.

I hope these elders will tell us what to do. It's a useful default when stuck in indecision to seek advice from others outside of us. Perhaps we'll be provided with some instruction, so we don't need to draw upon our own resources.

"Ooh, what's happening here?"

The woman approaches with an interested tone.

"Do you have a mobile phone we could borrow to make an emergency call?" I ask.

"I'm sorry, we don't. Looks like nature will take its course here," she replies, as they continue to walk past the crow crime scene.

The inconvenience of this situation starts to grate on me and right there and then, the next move becomes clear.

"Ok, we're going to have to pick up this bird and take it with us back to the house," I say to the girls.

I take off my cashmere woollen jumper and use it to scoop up the emaciated, winged seabird we call 'Alba'. It's so light it's like lifting air. I'm worried I'll crush it with kindness. Alba struggles at first and tries to wriggle out of my grip, but I hold our feathered friend close to my chest and make a tight cocoon around its body. A minute goes by and I feel Alba surrender into stillness and sink deeply into the soft carrier, moving along with its rescue team up the beach.

"Mum, I'll run in front so I can get the phone quickly," Zoe yells into the wind. "I'm so happy Alba won't be eaten alive."

Huffing and puffing, we arrive at the back door of the rental house. Once I've found a cardboard box, I place Alba gently in the corner. Her eyes are closed but she is still breathing. I free my hands to make the call.

Luckily, a young man answers and we describe the situation and send through some photos of Alba. He advises us that the closest official person who can take care of Alba is in Torquay, which is an hour's drive away. At this point, I have forty-five minutes to pack up the house and check out, so I agree that Alba will come with us in the car for the journey on the way home. Zoe stays vigilantly next to the box, keeping track of Alba's vital signs. Piling the last bag into the boot, I shout at the girls to get in the car. Alba takes position in the centre of the backseat with a seatbelt wrapped across the box. Looking into the rear-view mirror, I notice that one eye blinks open as this bird of the ocean assesses its new foreign environment.

Well, this is a first, I think to myself.

Driving along the coastal winding road, I turn up the tunes and start singing along.

"This must be the first time Alba has heard music," I say to the girls.

Leila looks across at me from the front seat and says, "Umm, Mum, birds invented music first. Duh!"

Corrected and awake to my ignorance, I realise how far from nature my arrogance can sometimes take me. My beliefs and decisions are often shaped by our own superiority as a species. For now, Alba is silent, but I imagine this bird has a beautiful song. The bird does not prefer a restricted five-minute slot for a song on a streaming service or radio. Music is part of the bird's creation to ensure not only its survival and a means to attract a mate, but a way to make beauty for beauty's sake. I imagine this charming creature is designed to sing and be heard. I hope there is still a verse left inside Alba and that it will form part of its healing story. I hope its wings won't be clipped of life's magic. As we approach Torquay for the handover, I drive into the side street at the arranged pickup point. An official-looking woman with an animal carrier gets out of her car and we meet on the side of the pavement. We exchange about five words before she looks into the box and picks up Alba for the next leg of the pilgrimage.

"Ahh, it's a shearwater sea eagle," she states with assertiveness. "C'mon, little buddy, let's go. Thanks! See you later!"

The three of us stand there looking at an empty box and exhale a sigh of relief.

"Mum, I know I'm definitely going to be a vet when I grow up now," Zoe says with confidence.

"Great, let's go home."

I told this story when I was leading a retreat once in Byron Bay, teaching a workshop on the different kinds of intuition. It was a peculiar time in my life when I was creatively blocked and had not yet started writing this book. The stories were all bound up inside me like a pretzel and I was constipated with ideas that couldn't find the flow. Perhaps the meaning of Alba's story was about how terrified this tiny creature was, and yet it still found its way into the arms of three giant creatures rooting for its survival. Even when we can't hear our intuition or feel completely stuck, we can trust that our survival instincts will take over and choose life every time. Even when we're being eaten alive by predators, real or imagined, there's a chance it's not our soul's time yet to depart. Even when our wings are clipped and we're too afraid to fly, we can trust that it's safe to fall into the arms of a greater power and let ourselves be carried for once.

Last Christmas Eve, I arrived at my in-laws' beach house and was given another bird sign. I was walking up the driveway and discovered a dead baby parrot lying on the concrete stone slab. It was tiny, about the size of my palm. Perhaps it was blown out of its nest in the treetops of one of the tall gums and plunged to its death below. I could hear bird cries above and wondered if its mother was desperately calling its name. Unable to survive the windy weather, I looked at its bald blue body on the ground, frozen without feathers. Maybe it jumped and tried to fly too soon? It struck me that I am utterly vulnerable to every creature on Earth, and they are vulnerable to me. In the same way butterflies remember being thin-skinned caterpillars, big creatures never forget their littleness. We're all growing and learning at the pace of trust. These are the reasons we need to stay in the nest until we're ready to spread our wings. So we can nurture our charm to withstand the outside forces. Creativity is a process and requires patience and staying power.

Before that retreat in Byron Bay, I invoked the power of Saraswati and prayed, *'You got to help me out, babe. I got nothing. Please bless me with the wisdom of creative flow and intelligence. Help me get out of my own way. Let me be ok with making mistakes and throwing control out the window. Thanks, I'd really appreciate it.'*

Saraswati directed me towards the water. *"Go get in the ocean,"* she instructed. In accepting an invitation to go down to the ocean in the dark to dip my soft animal flesh in the cold sea before sunrise, I met by happenstance, a group of women, and we were brave together. A bunch of like-minded local water babes seeking something beyond themselves. Amongst them was a woman who also happened to be an author. It only took a few minutes of chatting for me to share with her that I'd had a massive writer's block for a year.

She said, "What are you waiting for? A fancy invitation? You're not that important. You're just like me. If you don't write, you will die of apathy and depression. Do you want to be dead?" *Boom.* I don't know if it was the icy temperature, the salt on my skin or my fear of sharks, but suddenly I felt mobilised. There come points in your life when you simply kick the back door open and break through. Life always sneaks in this entrance when we least expect it. A total change of heart or perspective ... and in blows the muse.

She saw me. And I saw her.

This is the connection all us humans need to spark our own true nature. When we attune to our original charm, the spark of inspiration is reflected back to us by others. We receive direct access to our unique overflowing ocean of creativity. We are all just swimming each other home.

Mary Oliver writes, *"The most regretful people on earth are those who felt the call to creative work, who felt their own creative power restive and uprising, and gave to it neither power nor time."* Many people have limited beliefs when it comes to creativity. We are conditioned to think that it only refers to the arts and pursuits such as music, drawing and theatre. However, how we dress, cook, garden, communicate and walk is creative. Even every breath we take is an act of creation as new cells appear and old cells drop off. You may have been taught that creativity is something you have to work hard at and slog away to access, or that it is hidden somewhere with your life purpose. However, creative charm is not a struggle to be endured. It's a wild adventure and wants to come out every chance it can.

Creative energy and spiritful energy are one and the same thing. It is about having an idea or inspiration and then bringing it into physical form. We make something out of seemingly nothing. Our intuition is our co-creative companion. Our unique individual charm means that no two creative contributions can be exactly the same. However, if you don't say yes to being the vessel through which this idea wants to come to fruition, the energy or information will find another vessel. Some say that creative inspiration pours itself into the containers that we are. If there is no room in our container, or we are not brave enough to take a leap on the idea, the idea finds another container to pour itself into. Because there is only one consciousness, there's no such thing as original thought, only original expression. Nobody has your background of stories or sees life through your lens or filter. Therefore, the way this seedling is nurtured and fertilised will become your craft. If you ever felt like your ideas have been stolen, or it's been done already, or you're procrastinating on starting a project, there is a disconnect from your charm and an underlying fear that is causing hesitation. The energy centre in the body that is designed to parent this process is the sacral chakra. On its journey towards the Earth, it needs to travel and overcome our fears around incarnation such as:

- I can't afford to do this
- My family will reject me
- It's too much work
- I don't have time

Living your intuition is agreeing to be a participant of the creative laws of the Universe. When you are not being your creative charming creature, when you are trying to act perfect or just survive, you are feeding a false decision maker and believing a false narrative that is full of excuses. It's a significant step up not to be the passive victim in a relationship with life. Instead of believing that everything is happening to you, shift to: *I have the power to manifest and be a participant in the paradigm of creation.*

The opposite of creativity is survival. It occurred to me that if I'm privileged enough not to be in survival mode and living meal to meal, then it is my responsibility to bring forth inspiration and embody the artist archetype. When we are safe enough to 'respond with ability' then we have the power of choice.

It is a choice to nourish your creative charm. It's more about taking things off to make space rather than putting things on.

While I wrote this book, nourishment looked like:
- Slowing down
- Rest
- Metabolising grief
- Ocean dips
- Travel to new places
- Pleasure in pasta
- Breathwork
- Yoga Nidra
- Flow writing
- Shaking
- Saunas
- Singing
- Walking

I made a significant decision to nourish my intuition on a daily basis and sit with this question ...

How can I create a charming life?
My creativity needed this radical soul shake-up. It was the catalyst for getting over the boulder in the middle of my spiritual path that blocked me from writing this book. It also made me want to be more of a participant in the collective to see what is possible when communities gather with shared intention and positive connection.

A creative journey may be compared to catching a new wave. In Rick Reubin's book, *"The Creative Act"*, he defines a new wave as an artistic new movement that transports you into a new era. Originating in French film in the 1960s, followed by the music scene in the seventies and eighties, it is now calling for a modern spiritual revolution. No matter what stories you tell yourself, you are an artist because you are the co-creator of your life. It's your way of being in the world that is creative.

We all have this potential inside us to change course, to reinvent, to express ourselves authentically and to create a ripple effect that inspires others. Intuition arrives in creative waves. These insights can be received in the depths of quiet stillness or in the flow of a new wave. Sometimes we read the tides and move gracefully with the current, and other times, we decide to paddle hard in opposition.

A new wave requires you to:
- Throw out the rule book of your storied self to become the transformed self.
- Cut chords with past protective beliefs, rigid overthinking, habitual patterns and unconscious fear-programming.
- Play with possibility, truth and honest desire without the undertow of self-doubt.
- Trust that the ultimate breakthrough for freedom is felt by leaving the world of 'always' and heading into the world of *new*.

Starting a personal movement is really just you finally owning the infinite depth of your love at last. You are *choosing* to become enchanted with yourself and live your intuition.

That all sounds great, but what if you're still feeling stuck?

What if you've done everything 'right' and you're still creatively blocked?

Sometimes 'stuck' is just a call to stop what you are desperately doing. I remember trying desperately to make a baby and fall pregnant, doing all the things so it would happen according to my strict schedule. After a year of relentless efforting and 'calendar sex', by my thirtieth birthday I gave up, announced that I was infertile and went out to buy and smoke a whole packet of cigarettes. The next month, I fell pregnant. Have you experienced something similar?

You're brushing up against your creative potential but can't quite access it.
- You are taking all the vitamins but unable to heal or energise.
- You are going to bed early and still waking up tired.
- You are following all the marketing rules and still can't sell.
- You are meditating an hour a day and can't manifest anything.
- You are getting no support or attention from your partner, despite your efforts to connect.

The mind will look at all of this as a problem to solve. It will make up reasons for why 'it' is not working, which usually results in *you* becoming the problem. In this narrative, *'There must be something wrong with me.'*

On the other hand, soul says, *'You are exactly where I want you.'*

Our souls can smell fear, and if fear is in the driver's seat trying to control the forwards momentum, creativity will not happen. It's the perfect system of universal protection. A soul will not negotiate with fear. It will pause all guidance and creative inspiration until you surrender.

How do you navigate this?
- Stop being a 'human doing' and consciously return to 'human beingness.'
- Go find the fear.

Clearing the unconscious, fearful belief that 'my way has to be the right way' is one of the greatest gifts of your intuition. It will remind you that letting go of control and trusting in the flow again is possible. Let life carry you.

·········· PRACTICE BREATHWORK ··········

NADI SHODHANA

WHAT IS ITS CHARM?

This is a yogic pranayama technique which balances both hemispheres of the brain while switching between nostrils. Nadis are the rivers or energy channels that run through us and there are around 72,000 of them. The nadis we focus on here are the left nostril, Ida (feminine), and the right nostril, Pingala (masculine). When we breathe through our left nostril, it slows down the nervous system and activates the right side of our brain which is our creative and intuitive hemisphere. When we breathe through the right nostril, it wakes up the nervous system and activates the left side of our brain which is our analytical and logical hemisphere. The charm of alternating through both nostrils is in its ability to restore balance. For our creative juices to flow, we need the right amounts of ease. For direction and structure, we need the right amount of motivation. Balancing the brainwave states, from thinking Beta waves to calm Alpha waves, creates these optimal conditions.

THE TYPE OF FEAR IT LOVES
Letting go of control.

HOW DO I DO IT?

1. Start in a comfortable seat, sitting up straight.
2. Place your index finger and middle finger between your eyebrows with your right hand and relax your left hand in your lap. You can put a bolster across your legs and use it to support your elbow.
3. Close your eyes and gently close your right nostril with your thumb. Inhale through your left nostril for four seconds.
4. Close the left nostril with the ring pinkie finger and release the right thumb to open the right nostril. Breathe out through the right nostril for four seconds.
5. With the right nostril still open, inhale for four seconds, then close it with your thumb.
6. Release your ring and pinkie finger to open the left nostril and exhale for four seconds.
7. This is one round. Repeat ten times.

JOURNAL PROMPTS

1. How am I nourishing my creative soul?
2. What lack or depletion do I feel in my creative life?
3. What do I have in common with the person I judge the most?
4. What does my charming creature want to create?

Durga

CHAPTER 9

BE A PEOPLE DISAPPOINTER

Chakra:	Solar Plexus [Manipura]
Consciousness:	Waking State
Mantra:	Om Dom Durgayei Namaha
Location:	Abdomen, stomach, liver, upper intestines, pancreas gland
Element:	Fire
Challenge:	Fear 'I'm not enough'
Power:	Self-esteem, courage, inner strength, bravery, personal power
Breath:	Breath of Fire/Kapalbhati Pranayama

"Your job, throughout your entire life, is to disappoint as many people as it takes to avoid disappointing yourself."
—Glennon Doyle

It's 2.00 pm. I'm sitting in the back row of the classroom in the left-hand corner next to my friend Laura. I have all my new coloured pencils lined up on my desk that I received at my tenth birthday party the week before. I hope that we get to draw next or create some art. That inspiration quickly fades as Mr Edge stands at the front of the room, his white, stained shirt struggling to stay buttoned over a tight, bursting beer belly.

"Right. Correct these sentences on the blackboard. You have twenty minutes," he shouts.

The carpet shudders.

His red face and bulbous nose bead with sweat. He must have a skin condition. His face is becoming a deeper blue and his nose veins are now popping into purple.

So many lines of curly chalk writing make me squint, but I dare not admit that I can't read it.

"Do you understand? I can't hear you!" he demands, met with nods and stammering.

"Yes, s-sir," a chorus cries.

Looking satisfied with his instructions, Mr Edge's face shifts to stare at Laura and I. He narrows his eyes. He walks towards us, and I feel the booming vibration of his heavy footsteps thundering past the desks until he's no longer in sight.

My shoulders freeze up around my ears and my breath disappears. I distract myself by singing in my head, *'Somewhere over the rainbow'* to force an immediate inhale back into my lungs.

Clang, clang. The sound of the belt buckle is right on time.

Clang, clang, click, claaaang.

Laura and I bow our heads down at our desks, sensing his presence. He's standing right behind us, three inches away. A stench of stale meat pie lingers in my nostrils. It's like a monster is hiding under the bed, except it's our teacher and it's not a bedtime story.

The zip. God, no.

I can hear him undo his trousers and shove his hands down his pants, adjusting himself. I imagine he is tucking in his shirt again? It's always after lunch, and always hovering over Laura and I. I wonder why he doesn't take his pants down in the bathroom during the break and why we have to be so close to it every single day. I don't know the reasons why this disturbs me. It makes no sense. The sound of his hands busily rummaging makes me feel so sad and sick. I never utter a word. I wait for his next move by bracing my stomach and gripping tightly onto my coloured pencils. I'm trapped in a classroom and stuck to a hard wooden chair like wet glue. I hope silence and pretending I'm invisible will make him stop, but it does not. All the children in the rows ahead take the same vow of quietude while we hear the echo of the metal belt buckle. I can't seem to shake that rattling in my merry-go-round head, the creak of the leather strap being pulled and tightened.

The air rushes behind my neck as he turns around and extends his poking hand towards us.

"Gotcha third rib," he jokes, as his fat fingers jab the side of our school dresses, pretending to tickle us around the bra line.

He looks at my chest again, and grins to show me his yellow, stubby teeth. He keeps his fingers touching at the level of my singlet behind my back. Circles them round and round a bit.

I can't run or hide, so I freeze a smile on my face and pretend to giggle to appear to be 'in' on the joke. The classroom is filled with frozen smiles.

Playing the game and literally pleasing the pants off this person is a routine practice. I don't want to upset him or see him angry. He got really mad once during maths and punched a boy in the face, giving him a big, black, bruised eye. I felt bad for the boy.

"You have finished all the exercises on the board, then? Good girls! Good girls get gold stars," he states.

To be good is the goal. I look over my shoulder at Laura beside me.

"Can I borrow your eraser?" I whisper.

She nods and slides it across to me.

I frantically start to rub out my mistakes on the page, realising I've done it all wrong. I'm scared to ask for help, so look across at Laura's work as she is already finished, copying out what my brain cannot process in a panic. I sit up a bit straighter and brush my mousey-brown fringe back off my face, hoping to appear more good. I am aching for a gold star. I look across the aisle and watch Mr Edge poke the side ribs of Sally. She has three gold star stickers proudly displayed on her desk. She flicks her head to the side with perfect pig tails, and rehearsed giggles while he tickles and runs his hand up the back of the zip line on her tunic. Her golden curls bounce and satisfy his gaze. He bends over her while staring intensely down her front. His heaving breath can be heard from the back of the room. He reaches into his pocket and pulls out the sheet of stickers.

"You've answered all the questions before anyone else. Another gold star for you, Sally!" he exclaims, while using his chalky thumb to press it onto her forehead.

Years later, I learn that Mr Edge was disbarred from teaching. Soon after that, I hear he died. I have no emotional reaction. Just a sense of that is about right.

"You cannot be afraid to disappoint people. You have to live the life you want to live. Sometimes, that means being the motherfucker who can put a middle finger up to everyone in the room and be totally comfortable with that."

—David Goggins

Wake up in the morning and ask yourself, *who can I disappoint today?*

Because up until now, the only person you've been disappointing is yourself.

We lose power from our third chakra when we feed the unconscious fear that 'I'm not enough'. We spend a lot of our energy overcompensating, and it's why we're exhausted.

Disappointing people is part of a healthy-lived life. If you're connected to your intuition, you will let people down. You can't live a life in integrity and keep everyone happy at the same time. You can't have it both ways. Disappointing people doesn't mean you've done something wrong or caused harm intentionally.

It is our cultural conditioning and programming which makes us believe we need to be a good girl at all costs. Good-girl programming sends a definitive message: *don't disagree.* It's why I hear so many women, when asked what they want, respond breezily with, "I don't mind. I'm easy."

Except that your intuition does mind. It cares very much about what you want and need to express, regardless of whether it comes across as difficult, or too much, or far from easy. Being a polite or nice person is the opposite of being a spiritually mature and responsible adult. In fact, the disease to please, to be good, easy, agreeable and keep the peace where our intuition is constantly shut down, damages our health. It is the compulsion to look after the emotional needs of others, while ignoring our own, which causes illness. It's why so many women tolerate the disconnection from their charming creature.

Easy is deadly. Chronic illnesses, disease, depression, insomnia, and addiction all stem from being the easiest person in the room and forgoing your own need for self-respect.

Play it safe, don't disappoint, work to fit in, and *earn your worth* were the messages I internalised in my childhood, and wow, did they set me back and make things harder than they needed to be.

When we turn two years old, the word most commonly spoken is 'No'.

Why did nature design us this way?

Why is this language universally programmed for toddlers?

Nature's agenda is that we all develop into independent human beings that can thrive unattached with our own sets of values, desires and esteem. If we don't ever feel safe to say 'no', then we have no reason to survive because we'll agree with anyone who may intend to cause us harm. If we can't say 'no', then our 'yes' doesn't have any meaning.

When we say 'no', we say 'yes' to ourselves, which reinforces our existence and reason for being here. It is communicating to our soul that *'yes' you can count on me for fulfilling my life assignment. I agree to the terms of my unique expression to be self-realised.* Only from this position can we really lead others to become self-actualised. Adults can cope with disappointment. Contrary to societal pressures and 'fitting in', you're under no obligation to make everyone's life comfortable and easy by being agreeable. Your role is not to avoid conflict or anger, but to learn how to communicate your feelings effectively when your boundaries have been crossed. This may bring up fear in other people and they will project their own insecurities and judgements onto you. It's not personal.

Part of learning to de-personalise disappointment will help us reverse the repression. Taking other people's reactions personally is a risky game to play. We can't control how others react, so it is much healthier for us to focus on controlling our own response. We are too often told anger is an unhealthy emotion, but when someone or something has betrayed your soul, anger is a natural response. It's a source of energy that can wake you the fuck up and help you realise that what you experienced was not right. It can turn fear into courage, intuition into action, and snap you out of a spell so you can fly out of the open cage.

Have your boundaries ever been violated by another person, and you didn't speak up, or suppressed what you were really feeling?

Our bodies know. Our intuition knows. Women are blessed and burdened with the ability to sense ill will. Our soul tells us when we're unsafe and being violated.

It's humiliating to admit this, but I still buy into our culture's standards of seeking male attention.

- I dye my long hair blonde to cover the mousey brown and greyness.
- I have pretended to enjoy talking about sport at finals parties.
- I've praised men who are less qualified than me in the workplace and watched them own my ideas.
- I've accepted alcoholic drinks from men when I don't want to drink.
- I've believed male spiritual gurus have more power and signed up to their courses.

I am awake to all the ways I've internalised lifetimes of conditions that oppress women and benefit men in this way. It's a worthy practice to own the power of our bodies and honour them in all their shapes, colours and sizes, not as the property of men, but as something holy and sacred. Consent is a function of intuition, which is the opposite of passively seeking the approval of men or authority figures and then wrongly relaxing in that illusion.

Through disapproval, internalised shame and lack of safety and support, children learn to be afraid of authority figures, teachers and parents. They then seek their approval, wanting to please them, so they are not abandoned or rejected. They need these *big* people to stay alive!

Over time, as we 'grow up' these patterns of behaviour become part of our people pleasing personality.

Gabor Mate says, *"The personality is an adaptation. What we call the personality is often a jumble of genuine traits and conditioned coping styles, including some that do not reflect our true self at all but rather the loss of it."* Saying 'yes' when it's a 'fuck no' inside is not healthy. The inability to say 'no' is a trauma response. Maybe someone asked your opinion or advice about something, and you gave them what you thought they wanted to hear, not what was honestly true for you. Or perhaps decisions were being made around you which affected your life directly and you were unable to ask for what you want and need. This drains our power and deflates our spirit when we can't fully express our intuition.

The questions we can ask ourselves are:
- What do I miss out on in life as a result of my inability to assert myself?
- What must I believe about myself to deny my own needs this way?
- Do I want an adult life?
- What would my adult life look like?

As a child, I became very good at sensing how other people felt and could stay one step ahead in anticipation of their reactions. It conditioned me to make up a narrative and believe in the story that ... my life works better when everyone else is happy. I cannot bear to see others suffer, so I must be responsible for how other people feel and what they experience. I must be a good girl and not disappoint!

When you are too externally focused on other's reactions, you lose touch with your inner voice. The result is often self-loathing and shame that follows when you're not capable of standing in your power and protecting yourself in the moment, or seeking recognition and not trusting your own truth.

Don't wait for others to validate your ideas and thoughts. Have the courage to say *this is not working for me*. And find your own way. You are not responsible for your partner's or your bosses' emotional reactions.

I've had to whisper to my inner eight-year-old, *'Hey, guess what, I'm forty-four now. I'm safe, even when other people don't like my choices.'*

"It actually doesn't take much to be considered a difficult woman. That's why there are so many of us."
—Jane Goodall

PRACTICE BREATHWORK

BREATH OF FIRE

WHAT IS ITS CHARM?

Our solar plexus is our most powerful centre for self-esteem. This practice is a pranayama practice and is an adaptation of kapalabhati commonly done in yoga. It clears stagnant energy quickly by activating the sympathetic nervous system for an extended period. Through pumping the belly and forcing the exhale, it has the potential to create heat, hence the fire, which you stoke with fast exhales through the nose. Fire is the element of transformation.

Ancient Tibetans used this technique, traditionally called 'tummo', to survive freezing mountain conditions.

The charm of this practice is in its destruction. It eliminates, through activating the diaphragm, anything blocking your 'not enoughness'.

Afterwards, you are left with a sensation of confidence and calm. Do this breath before you need to set a boundary, say yes or no, or potentially disappoint someone. It's especially useful in the morning to wake up, before an important meeting to increase alertness or when you need to make a clear decision.

THE TYPE OF FEAR IT LOVES
The belief 'I'm not enough'.

HOW DO I DO IT?

1. Start in a seated, cross-legged position. Sit up tall.
2. Place your hands on your knees, palms facing upward. You can also place a hand on your belly to feel it rise as you breathe.
3. Inhale through your nose, feeling your belly expand as you do so.
4. Without pausing, exhale forcefully through your nose while contracting your abdominal muscles. Keep your inhales and exhales equal in length. Repeat until you're comfortable with the pattern.
5. Continue the rhythm, inhaling passively and exhaling forcefully. Repeat several times to practise.
6. Now speed up the inhales and exhales. Your exhales should be powerful and loud.
7. Repeat for thirty seconds or forty-four times.

   Over time, you can try doing the Breath of Fire for longer.

JOURNAL PROMPTS

1. Where in my life am I blocking my own power?
2. In what area of my life do I feel most powerful?
3. Who am I waiting to get approval from?
4. What is the cost of hustling for this validation?

Kuan Yin

CHAPTER 10

HIMALAYAN HEARTWORK

Chakra:	Heart [Anahata]
Consciousness:	Transcendental
Mantra:	Om Mani Padme Hum
Location:	Heart, lungs, shoulders, ribs, breasts, thymus gland
Element:	Air
Challenge:	Fear of rejection
Power:	Compassion, gratitude, forgiveness, abundance, beauty
Breath:	Conscious Connected Breathwork

"Biology is the least of what makes someone a mother."
—Oprah Winfrey

The taste of death and dust lingers in the back of my throat. I swallow the metallic tang over my tongue. I always knew I'd go to Nepal but am surprised on the first day of landing that I'm standing at the cremation ghats where a charred body burns in front of me on concrete slabs. There are fires and flames, five of them, rising towards the heavens. Everything I see, hear, smell and touch is humming with contrasting aliveness and a haze which could also be brain fog. It's hard to believe that forty-eight hours earlier I was on the other side of the world making pizzas for my kids' dinner. Am I dreaming or is this jet lag? Shock therapy is the medicine for being present with what's right here.

I am about to lead a retreat with one of my co-hosts Tuuli. Before our guests arrive, she takes me to this place, Pashupatinath. This centre of Hinduism is lined with crumbling temples that reflect the essence of impermanence. It's a culture and temple she likes to visit again and again with visitors to experience through new eyes. It is believed after visiting this holy Pashupatinath area that your soul, body and wealth have become holy and sacred. I am all in.

The whole area is bursting with tourists and locals. Life and death collide as overpowering polarities. A combination of both peace and chaos on either side of the river offers a continuous picture of colour and sights through every physical sense. The mayhem of Kathmandu echoes in my ears and sends a waft of spicy incense-smoked flesh up my nose. The message is clear. Throw everything and its opposite together and declare it all sacred and worthy of love.

A group of three men, mostly naked and covered in ash and red paste, sit nearby, getting ready for the procession. Matted dreadlocks and scarves wrapped round their heads, the sadhus stand to carry the next corpse on a bamboo stretcher towards the holy waters on its final pilgrimage along the dung-splattered river. These extreme renunciates, eyes laser sharp, poke the blue cadaver and ready its transition with shaking bells and escalating chants. Laying the body upon stacks of fired charcoal wood, they manhandle all the shrivelled parts to ensure it all burns completely. I can't help but wonder how the locals feel about their loved one's funeral being a tourist attraction.

Sadhus choose to liberate themselves from the material world and be at one with ash and cremation. These ghats are their home. Their Vedic scriptures say if they are cremated there, they'll break the cycle of birth and rebirth and attain enlightenment or moksha. This is their service. I silently nod to the death passing me by, aware of the sound of my own breath and signs of life loudly exhaling.

What brings up the raw emotion in me the most is not the wails of grief crying, but the overwhelming expressions of celebration, dancing, gratitude and joy as souls depart. When I lock eyes with one of the holy men, he grins back. I smile at him and stare at his kind face, feeling a wave of love flow through my next breath. I sense his blessing of encouragement, like, "You are in the right place!"

I've arrived two days before the rest of my retreat group to get accustomed to this new landscape beckoning exploration.

Before I lead any retreat, I'm familiar with this vulnerable sense of doubt and anticipation that I don't have what it takes to even begin. It's classic imposter syndrome that tries to crush my spirit. Combine that with being in a foreign country for the first time and my heart begins to quiver. I recognise it immediately as fear of doing the work of the goddess. It's a visceral reaction that is still deep in my DNA from being persecuted lifetimes ago for empowering the work of witches. I now know to expect this imposter to show up right on schedule.

Exhaling slowly, the wise self confronts the rogue woman imposter.

'Ahh, yes, there you are, on time as always, forty-eight hours before. Now, how do you want to work this? Shall I ask you to leave quietly, or do you want to be dragged kicking and screaming?'

Placing a hand over my heart and taking three deep breaths, I tune back into the charm and the intuition that plugs me into my bigger why. The rogue woman backs down and my soul opens a conversation with the goddesses.

'Please help me remember I'm being supported, and all is going

according to divine plan. Every fibre of my being is ready to receive this group and the transformations that await us.'

Immediately, I notice signs of devotion circling this holy attraction. Deity images recognisable from my yoga books and sacred texts are everywhere. I see pictures of creatures, the tiger of Durga, the big elephant head of Ganesha guarding doorways, Kali's long red tongue on tourist t-shirts, Saraswati's swan, Kuan Yin's lotus, Shiva's serpent on statues and pink-bummed stuffed monkeys hanging off wires. Closer to the temples, I observe nuns in robes, wild artwork with furious representations of the war within each one of us battling light and dark, and pilgrims prostrating with paddles under their hands pushing themselves through pain thresholds.

There are buildings in a labyrinth of alleyways and tall rooftops, incredibly linked with electricity wires that resemble spaghetti tangles. The presence of worship extends even on the infrastructure. Buddha under the tree, Buddha lying down, Buddha with a big belly, and the 'big boss's' eyes on top of the infamous Boudhanath Stupa, inviting every visitor to awaken the Buddha inside. There's a very active humming in the atmosphere and I join in under my breath, hum hummm hummmmm.

After an hour, we both are ready to leave, with senses exploding and persistent monkeys beginning to hone in.

"Let's go and get some dinner," Tuuli suggests.

"Yes, great idea," I reply, while carefully clutching my sunglasses and phone away from cheeky, swinging creatures.

I'm grateful to continue the initiation and we make our way through the crowds and back onto the clear road to Boudhanath Stupa.

Walking around the Stupa temple in a clockwise direction, monks pray and meditate with their malas, peacefully spinning prayer wheels as they pass by on purpose. I join the circle and shuffle into line, hoping to board the peace train while muttering mantras.

The air is so thick with repeated rolling 'Oms' it's hard to feel lonely, even in a place that is so 'otherworldly'. In the Buddhist tradition, it's the word Bodhicitta that describes loving-kindness for all sentient charming creatures. As demonstrated by Siddhartha Gautama (Buddha), it's also embodied by Kuan Yin as the feminine Goddess of mercy and compassion whose cries for the world can be heard in her mantra 'Om Mani Padme Hum'. The sound 'Om' is believed to be the primordial sound of creation. The 'Ma' in Mani dissolves attachment to fleeting pleasures. 'Pad' in Padme empties us of judgement, and 'Hum' lets go of aggression and hatred. As I imagine my lotus flower blooming out of the mud, I wonder, *how can one not go straight to heaven with this soundtrack constantly playing on your tongue?* I like to think I'm upgrading with some new spiritual software into my circulation system.

"Om Mani Padme Hum," I chant.

I see the symbols of this mantra inscribed in Sanskrit on surfaces of souvenirs. When chanted out loud, I'm repeating sounds which reverberate through millions of mouths every minute of every day. This collection of syllables for compassion translates to 'The jewel in the lotus'. This phrase suggests we all have the lotus flower within us; sometimes it's just covered in mud. The Dalai Lama believes it has the power to *"transform your impure body, speech and mind into the pure body, speech and mind of a Buddha."*

After completing one lap of the Stupa, we begin to walk down an alley towards a side street, making our way to the restaurant. In contrast to the joy and high spirits, a woman walks up to me, begging while breastfeeding her baby. She extends an arm out to me, and her fingernails are black with dirt. She's wearing a red sari over an old t-shirt and her hair is long and scraggly.

"Please, money? Rupees, dollars?" she asks.

I can't look and I can't turn away, either.

Told not to give beggars anything, it perpetuates a cycle of poverty and harm that benefits nobody. Mothers will cut off their child's arms to achieve this tragic effect in exchange for business. And so, I smile forcedly and say, "Namaste". It's a weird response as I notice the dangers she is facing, including contaminated water, disease and hunger.

Not sure where to look, I find strength from a quote I had written down in my journal by culture journalist Pico Iyer, *"Many people one meets while traveling deal with more traumas every day than the privileged among us meet in a lifetime. That's how travel humbles and inspires."*

I wonder whether my unearned privilege of being born into a wealthy country makes my being here an indulgence? Or might the absence of visitors lead to a lack of resources and much needed economy? I see how interacting with marginalised communities is strengthening my appreciation of what in life is essential.

I see people living on the street bow, often smiling with craggy teeth, saying, "Namaste". The elders have fascinating face lines, each telling a story. They make their way reverently towards the next ceremony.

It just raises more questions.

Why is a sacred pilgrimage important and why do people repeat it for thousands of years?

Why is retreating into other cultures a calling for me?

I don't know the answers but am prepared to live the questions for the next ten days.

The next morning, I wake at five o'clock to the next door monastery's vibration of beating drums. My head is surprisingly free of jet lag. A group of ten women gather in the hotel foyer to meet for the first time. They're all from Melbourne and say the same thing when I ask, "Why did you book this?"

"I don't know. I just knew I had to be here," was the collective response.

Roman, our Nepalese guide, interrupts the introductions and non-stop excited chatter, barely able to get a word in edgewise.

"Good morning. Pokhara is waiting for us. Jum jum," he shouts joyfully.

We translate that to meaning time to hop on the bus.

After our bus ride, we wait to board our light aircraft, which will deliver us to the first trekking village. Each day on this hike will draw us closer to the holiest mountain in the Annapurna ranges, called Machapuchare or Fishtail Mountain. It is believed to be the Himalayan home of Lord Shiva and the highest in spirit at seven thousand metres tall. An unclimbable, untouchable, unshakeable, sacred mountain. Himalaya means the <u>alaya</u> (home) of <u>hima</u> (snow). The story goes that one day two Norwegians and two sherpas set off and climbed within fifty feet of the summit but never returned. The lesson is a reminder that we're not here to conquer the top of the peaks. Human nature knows its place as tiny creatures, even if the human ego does not. The minute I step off the plane, the whipped frenzy of a heavy, populated city begins to fade. No smoke or sadhus here, just devoted mountain walkers and purists seeking something transcendent.

To get from Pokhara Airport to our first home for the evening, we drive around cliff edges on a one-way road for a long time. There are no other vehicles on the road. I wouldn't even call it a road because it did not resemble anything smooth or flat or functional. It is late afternoon, and the cloud cover is starting to blanket across the sky. Bouncing up and down on the back seat of the jeep, holding onto my sister next to me for support, I glimpse a sign.

Welcome to Astam Eco Village.

Multi-coloured prayer flags, lightly snapping in the breeze, welcome our arrival at our first night's stay as we pull up at its entrance.

I'm given an ancient looking key and make my way to the guest house where I flop gratefully onto my bed, bursting to guide the first breathwork class. Out my window, a huge full moon rises above the valley and lights up the entire sky. Infinite, sparking moonbeams make it difficult to close my eyes. I don't mind being awake with a belly full of home-grown vegetarian food. Then I breathe, and the mountains breathe, setting the cosmos in sleepy motion once again.

In one day's travel, we are a thousand years away.

"Just as a white summer cloud, in harmony with heaven and earth freely floats in the blue sky from horizon to horizon following the breath of the atmosphere—in the same way the pilgrim abandons himself to the breath of the greater life that ... leads him beyond the farthest horizons to an aim which is already present within him, though yet hidden from his sight."

—Lama Govinda

On our first morning in the mountains, I open my eyes before first light. I peep out at the silent universe. God is not even awake yet. Dawn is teasing me out of my room to let some sunlight into my heart. The anticipation around whether the clouds are covering the snowcaps or not is the game of hide and seek we play with the Himalayas each morning. Halos of white wisps spin in vanilla soft serve whorls around each pinnacle, holding all the secrets until they are ready to lift the curtain. There, standing boldly before us, is the first glimpse of Fishtail and no overcast weather in sight. It's like visual poetry. Snow cones are silhouetted against a sunrise and a blue sky so clear it almost hurts to look at. I can't believe this higher kingdom is forever uninhabited.

The group merges round, one by one stumbling out of their cosy rooms to salute the sight in front of them. Awe and wonder reverberate between us as worship seems the only attitude. As the light reflects at the exact moment in time when the angle of the sun hits the side of the mountains, we all gasp. Rocks rise into colossal points, broken up into shark's teeth. They look not of this Earth, and we are swallowed in the jaws of it, happy to be protected and ensconced inside its mouth.

We are torn between wanting to capture the picture on our phones forever and just standing in our own mountain pose, 'tadasana', being at one and savouring the experience of this glowing and glistening heavenly scene.

We set out for the morning to walk to our next village. The ten of us hike in pairs and trios of various formations, sometimes all of us in single file, making a festive Congo vibe of it or a silent mindful procession. Walking, by its very simplicity, knows how to move through complex issues. Every hike I trust myself, I forgive myself, I challenge myself and I connect with what matters. We pass other hikers and sherpas on the trail, quickly discerning the difference between pilgrims and professional porters. Sherpa is the Tibetan word for 'easterner' and are mostly local men. Carrying up to forty kilograms on their hunched backs, they haul a load balanced by a headgear strap around their foreheads. They look too light and slight for the load, but it's the way they carry it that is impressive. These people smile, and that is the greatest miracle of all.

At the edge of the path, we pass two giant yaks having just deposited some fresh cakes. The smell of sour buffalo milk mixed with manure waters my eyes. Nepalese women are seated on the sidewalks selling vegetables and beads, pounding grains in stone mortars and weaving threads of pashmina into beautiful shawls. I shouldn't be surprised that Wi-Fi is available before bottled water. This remoteness remains authentic only by adapting to modern needs.

Packs of wild, rangy dogs run free. Locals care for them and consider that one may even incarnate as their future child. Dogs are suggested to be revered creatures only one lifetime away from being human. One canine in particular takes a loyal interest in our group. This black labrador-like beauty has no apparent home address. She chaperones us on our hike, checks the trail ahead is clear, makes sure we stick together and ensures our safe arrival to the next village. Then she disappears into the hills. This creature is like a retreater's best friend, offering her pilgrims protection and unconditional love and expecting nothing in return. She is acting out her dharma. We call her Durga.

Goddess Kali is the goddess who leaps out of Durga's third eye when doing battle. Some days, Durga needs to draw on more power during the arc of a pilgrimage and the unexpected wars within us that we face. When evil, or fear, starts to multiply, it can get out of hand and our shadows start to clone themselves. Not only are we criticising ourself, but we notice we are now criticising and judging everyone. This is the sneaky work of the ego.

On this particular day, a Kali-like energy arrives, bringing to the surface a now-or-never opportunity. The limiting fearful stories all coming to the surface, bubbling up, joining forces and full speed with the group's shared human experience. Narratives spill out, perhaps being pulled by the gravitational force of our surroundings.

"I'm never good enough."
"I'm an outsider."
"I'm so angry."
"I can't carry this anymore."

I keep walking, huffing and puffing up the next hill, unable to switch off my own mind while the conversations swirled around each path.

The drop of spit landing on my face, girls laughing.

I keep walking.

A squeaking mouse, running near my head.

I breathe hard, focusing on the next step.

My daughter, incessantly exercising, a mirror of an anorexic me.

The top of the cliff is in view now.

Mr Edge behind me, unzipping his pants.

I reach the top of the cliff and sit on the rock, my inner children, controlling clipboard, invisible wounded and repressed anger, beside me. We are one hour to the next village and the words on the trail are mixed with silence and deep reflection. I wander up beside one retreater and we sink deeper into conversation.

"I feel like I'm one decision away from a new life, but I'm scared."

"What is your biggest fear?" I ask.

"I'll be alone," she replies.

"How old do you feel right now?" I ask.

"I'm ten years old. Fuck, I thought I dealt with all this shit," she exhales.

"We always have that charming child inside us. She'll never disappear. But is that wound going to keep you a little girl or are you going to grow up? I have a sense that your inner woman knows about being alone and has survived it many times," I respond, and at the same time feel like I'm talking to myself.

As we arrive in the next village, the wind picks up and Kali's presence is noted. The Goddess of transformation is clear with her instruction, and we settle onto our mats to begin a 'meet your shadow' workshop. It would be convenient if we could always stay looking at the light and never look at what is buried, but that's not Kali's gift of grace.

I recall this quote by author Anne Lamont, *"I wish grace and healing were more abracadabra kind of things. Also, that delicate silver bells would ring to announce grace's arrival. But no, it's clog and slog and scootch, on the floor, in the silence, in the dark."*

Once again, we get into the clog and slog as I guide the women in a meditation, lying on the floor of the hostel garden beside the public hiking trail. In the middle of meeting the victim shadow, I'm shocked at a sound that jolts me out of the imagined dungeon.

Is that sleigh bells ringing?

I turn around expecting to see seven reindeers trotting along with Santa behind them.

Instead, it's a herd of miniature donkeys with their brass bells jingling around their necks. Descending from the mountain on a melody of tunes, this pack train is following their shepherd joyfully while delivering goods to the next tea house.

Grace is here!

Hooves tap dance on the rocky ground. Right on cue, another serendipitous entry adds meaning to our own shadow dance. Mules, being muses, remind us that illumination is always present, even when we're in the darkness doing the inner work. The brilliant charm of the mountains always watching us, even when their peaks are concealed by the clouds.

These divine creatures jangling are on a mission, carrying the load lightly as if to offer us that wisdom, "It's not the weight of the load, it's how you carry it that matters in life."

Smiles creep across our faces in the Nepalese sherpa way. This is the greatest miracle of all. This is how we carry the load of life. There's an arc on a retreat for each individual that often leads to a peak moment of vulnerability and letting go of loaded baggage. I cherish the communal energy of these sacred turning points. Each day is another chance to share a ritual of spiritual transformation and retire happily exhausted when the stars come out. How we inhabit our vulnerability is directly proportionate to our willingness to be more intimate with our shadows. We descend spiritful and beautifully simplified, leaving behind one way of living and preparing for another. As Carl Jung said, *"One does not become enlightened by imagining figures of light but by making the darkness conscious. The brighter the light, the darker the shadow. Shadow work is the path of the heart warrior."*

"Vulnerability is not a choice. Vulnerability is the underlying, ever-present and abiding undercurrent of our natural state. To run from vulnerability is to run from the essence of our nature; the attempt to be invulnerable is the vain attempt to become something we are not and, most especially, to close off our understanding of the grief of others."

—Poet, David Whyte

To run from vulnerability is to run from your charm. The only way to live your intuition is to risk emotional exposure and embrace both the chaos and the calm of the unknown. It is purely the energy of the heart chakra that invites us to strip down the walls of protection guarding our feelings.

As mysterious as this kind of loving invitation is, it's not all about magic and miracles. This level of love wears hard-working boots. It stands sturdy beside you as you sit in the fear and live the brave question ...

Can I sit in this vulnerable space of not knowing what's next without freaking out or gripping onto control?

Through the transformative power of forgiveness and mercy, it journeys with you to the centre of your mountain. This love does not wipe your tears but wishes you would let them fall further and water new seeds. This love is also up for ugly crying, purging past pain and primal screaming.

Learning to recognise sadness, depression and disappointment as a necessary part of shadow work is part of the process. It is the charming children, the false parts of us that are sad. They are sad that the game is up. They are digging their heels in not wanting to move forward in the direction the invisible hand on your back is pushing you toward. It's a type of sacred sadness we need to accept and the price our soul pays to fall upwards into the light.

This level of vulnerability is not weakness. Vulnerability has been so feared and misunderstood as a weakness, as something to run away from at all costs. When we strip ourselves of our armour, we can only depend on what's left, and what remains is truth. There's nothing concealing us; no roles or masks, not someone else's formed opinions or beliefs about us. We are just as naked as the day we were born.

It takes enormous courage to die to yourself over and over again. The death that's required can't be underestimated as we burn the bridges, meaning we can never return to our previous way of existing. To let go and leave old versions and people behind. To redefine new conditions for your charming creature to thrive. To empower the charm in others and let them see you. Really see you.

As our retreat group recited the Ho'oponopono prayer over and over, while gazing into our partner's eyes, our words dissolved into one another as we witnessed vulnerability work its magic ...

> *"I'M SORRY,*
> *PLEASE FORGIVE ME,*
> *THANK YOU,*
> *I LOVE YOU."*

When a pilgrimage begins, we intentionally hold a schedule loosely. Intuition leads us to create space for magic. Not holding onto any plans is vulnerable. To leave our itinerary open to synchronicity and embrace serendipity. Discovering freedom from agendas and time constraints is counter to our cultural programming. It's vulnerable to embrace uncertainty as a kind of freedom. Rather than roles, routines and responsibilities dictating our days, we find that freedom shifts to brand new ways of existing. Instead of charting progress on a set timetable, we feel that progress with every step we take.

Travel lends itself to flow intuition. Not knowing what will happen next, not knowing the map, not knowing the people you will meet, not knowing the language is the brilliant recipe for meeting yourself again for the first time. I became attuned to new friendships, loud chanting, prolonged silences and more open to allow wonder and imagination to guide the days and nights. Absorbed in the sights, sounds and smells, you're just there as you are. French philosopher Simone de Beauvoir reflects on travel, *"I forget my own existence. I live in a moment that embraces eternity."*

Unexpectedly, something else unfolded during the Himalayan heartwork. I fell head over heels in love with my body, my flesh, just the way it is, and felt this sadness that it can't come with me when I take my last breath. Releasing all the fears around how I've rejected my body has been liberating. The times I condemned it for being too slow, too sick, too wrinkly, too scarred, too saggy, too fat, too thin, too white, too soft and too average.

I have punished my body for causing me pain, poured toxins down my throat, and treated it like a giant problem to be solved. Spinning a victim story from my mind instead of accepting that bodies do what bodies do. Bodies get sick, they heal, they decay and they die. It's not personal. Bodies also are our vehicle for strength, endurance, grace and pleasure.

In the book *"On Living"*, written by aged-care chaplain, Kerry Egan, she writes, *"There are many regrets and many unfulfilled wishes that patients have shared with me in the months or weeks before they die. But the time wasted spent hating their bodies, ashamed, abusing it or letting it be abused—the years, decades, or in some cases, whole lives that people spent not appreciating their body until they were so close to leaving it—are some of the saddest."*

I'll need to say goodbye to the legs that walk me around the world, this belly that birthed two children, this vessel that sleeps soundly at night and seeks adventure as soon as the sun rises. And with that has been a deepening gratitude for Tina and her temporary existence.

We pay a very high price for not loving our body and its vulnerability. Over and over, we abandon ourselves because we don't like this or that about ourselves and buy into an idealist culture that tells us our body is wrong. We never get to know the benevolent being that we are, and we're the only one who can do so. That price is too high for one wild and precious life. I had discovered a benevolence to my own breath. The preciousness of being in such high rare air and the unrelenting solid permanence of the mountains only seemed to emphasise my own fragility. It's pretty easy to find peace amongst the wild Earth in its natural environment, but can we let it emerge from us in all the reality of regular, round tables and relationships?

Ultimately, travel is not about expressing a worldlier persona or projecting your spiritual awakening onto others. It's about getting closer to who you are and redefining your values. When the retreat is over, what counts for more than gushing about how amazing it all was is showing how the experience has changed you. This is a homebound travel exercise that exists in sacred spaces around the kitchen bench, at our children's bedside, in the car and on Zoom meetings.

Being spiritful does not demand renunciation of ordinary life, just demonstration of an extraordinary one.

"When we were children, we used to think that when we were grown up, we would no longer be vulnerable. But to grow up is to accept vulnerability ... To be alive is to be vulnerable."

—Madeleine L'Engle

BIG LITTLE SISTER STORY
CHELLE MCQUAID

"What needs to be allowed to die?" Tina asked.

It was a big question for the first morning of our yoga retreat in

Nepal. But my heart's answer was immediate: my past selves.

Wait. What?

After a lifetime of denying them, I'd worked very hard over the last seven years to finally understand and accept all the different parts of myself. There was Fear who flapped her hands in circles when I was afraid, and Faith who found safe spaces for me to rest. There was Anxiety who made me fart (loudly), and Love who transformed my gas into bubbles of light. And there was Disgust who sucked in poisonous judgements about others, and Compassion who helped me spit out the poison and get curious about everyone's perfect imperfection. And a rag-tag bunch of other parts.

In the process of getting to know them, I'd grown very attached to my quirky little internal family—even the ones who were hard to love at first. Surely, now that we were finally all getting along, there was no need to kill any of them off.

"Tonight, we'll visit Pashupatinath where local bodies are cremated by the Bagmati River the day after death," Tina explained. "It can be an intense experience with the smell and ashes from the bodies burning. It's ok if you'd rather not come."

Phew. I can just opt out. Sounds like the safest option.

"It is entirely your choice," Tina said.

Darn it. I wrestled with my choice all afternoon.

When I reached for my journal, my heart was adamant: it was time to let them go. *Together, you have done the work, healed the past, and learned to find love and safety within yourself. You are all grown up. They want to be set free now, dear girl. If you are ready to let them burn tonight, then this is your opportunity. If you are not ready yet, they will wait. Just be in no doubt that at some point, this is the next step for your growth.*

At dusk, as I walked down towards the funeral pyres, I was still busy trying to buy myself more time. I couldn't believe it was time to say goodbye. We'd had a lifetime of adventures together. Who would I be without them? How would I go forwards?

As we sat on the riverbanks opposite the Pashupatinath Temple, we watched families lovingly tending to the bodies of their deceased relatives before gently setting them alight. There was no wailing or sounds of heartbroken sobbing. There was just a very quiet honouring of life.

Eventually, Tina said, "It's time to go."

I wasn't ready. But I wouldn't have been ready, even if I sat there all night.

As I followed Tina over the bridge and past the cremation grounds, my past selves gently whispered, 'It's time. We love you. We're so proud of you. Go and live a wild and beautiful life.'

Then, I felt them separate from my body and the energy of my past selves floated down the stairs to the burning funeral pyres. And the rest of me kept walking.

As we left the temple grounds, I tried to reassure myself that this was all just a crazy invention of my overactive imagination. Parts of ourselves don't separate from our bodies. Clearly, the smoke from the pyres was playing with my mind.

But as I searched around inside myself for those old parts, there was no denying that I could not feel them. For the first time ever, their voices were silent. They were gone. And like a lobster who sheds its old shell, I was left with the space for my new self to grow.

Dr Michelle McQuaid
– Wellbeing Researcher and the Founder of The Good Girl Game Changers

---

"A single breath has more truth in it than all your thoughts about breathing will ever have."
—Adyashanti

·········· **PRACTICE BREATHWORK** ··········

CONSCIOUS CONNECTED BREATHWORK

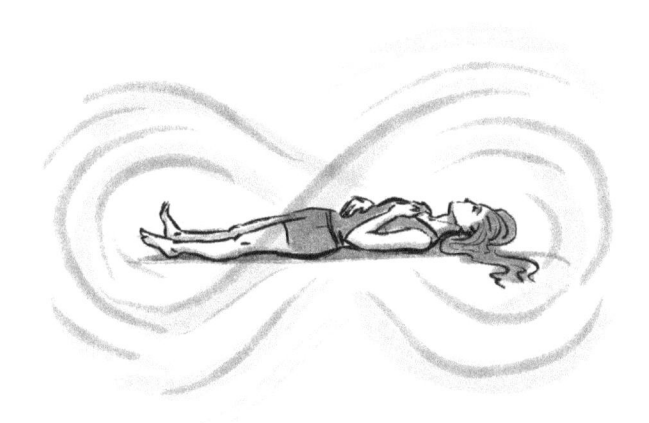

WHAT IS ITS CHARM?

This practice of Conscious Connected Breathwork (CCB) is also known as Rebirthing Breathwork. It brings a constant flow of energy into the body for the purpose of healing. Created by Leonard Orr in the 1970s, its therapeutic benefits are the most powerful I've ever experienced. Before I became a rebirthing facilitator, I resisted doing the training because I really believed as a yoga teacher I already knew everything about the breath. Boy, was I wrong. I love being wrong!

Its charm is in its power to release stored stress and layers of accumulated trauma. It's not uncommon to hear first-time students call their session the most spiritual experience they've ever had. They receive profound intuitive insights. At the same time, it teaches you how to stay grounded in the body and feel all the feelings and emotions that arise. The connected breath creates a circular electricity circuit which charges the body with energy. It moves intelligently through the parts where it is most useful to promote repair and clearing. It can create tingly, buzzy sensations, physical pain shifts, emotions, memories, love, visions, fears, spirit communications and mystical experiences that open a doorway to the subconscious. It embodies being both a human *and* a divine creature.

This practice supports the cultivation of compassion and forgiveness as it empties grief from the heart chakra. When we breathe connected, we plug ourselves back into Universal source, melting all illusions of fear and separation.

THE TYPE OF FEAR IT LOVES
Fear of rejection.

HOW DO I DO IT?

This practice can be done either sitting up or lying down. A longer session is lying down for up to ninety minutes with an experienced facilitator.

1. CCB simply involves eliminating the pause between the inhale and the exhale, breathing in and out of your nose in a continuous motion of breath. Nasal breathing has evidently many health benefits.
2. The basic technique is a circular pattern of breathing, where as soon as you reach the top of the inhale, you

exhale. Then, before finishing the exhalation, you inhale again, connecting one breath to the other.
3. The pace is slightly faster than normal, but without forcing or pushing.
4. If sitting up on your own, do three rounds of twenty with a minute to rest in between.
5. If being guided, ensure you are comfortable to breathe for an hour lying down and do not have any of the medical contraindications as outlined by your facilitator.

JOURNAL PROMPTS

1. If the goddess or unconditional charm had a voice, what would she say to you?
2. How does holding onto the past serve you?
3. Do you need to forgive yourself so you can be free?

This prompt is inspired by poet Andrea Gibson. Write a love letter from the part of your body that you love the least to the part of your body that you love the most or vice versa. What can that part teach the other part?

Kali

CHAPTER 11

TAKE RISKS

Chakra:	Throat [Vishudda]
Consciousness:	Cosmic
Mantra:	Om Kleem Kalikayei Namaha
Location:	Throat, thyroid gland, cervical neck, mouth, teeth, gums, jaw
Element:	Ether
Challenge:	Fear of authentic expression
Power:	Unlimited potential, inner ferocity, slaying egoic illusions
Breath:	Woodchoppers Breath/Lions Breath/Simha Pranayama

"The closer we get to a childlike state of free self-expression, the purer our test and the better our art."
—Rick Reubin

I'm walking home from school pickup with my youngest daughter and her friend, hurrying them along so we don't miss their basketball game at 4.00 pm.

"I don't want to play," my daughter moans.

"Why not?" I ask.

"I don't like the coach. He's too strict and it's not fun."

"Yeah," her friend chimes in. "He gets all up in your personal space, too."

"Well, he's just trying to get the best out of a bunch of grade four girls who chat and sometimes don't listen," I say quickly, while responding to an email on my phone. "He has lots of experience coaching."

Zoe stays silent and looks at the ground.

We have twenty minutes to get there. Rushing to get changed at home into uniform, we then run to the courts and make it just in time for the whistle to blow. Every parent is lined up along the sidelines. I sit down on the plastic chair and take a moment to breathe. My eyes follow the girls up and down the court, some focused and others looking airily into space. Zoe catches the ball and throws it into the hoop.

Whoosh. A goal! I clap and yell out, "Well done! Keep it going."

My feelings of joy quickly crash as Zoe is pulled off the game. A 'time out' is called. The coach stumbles and shakes his hands erratically while shouting aggressively at the children. Spit flies from his lips and lands on wide eyes. His hand stretches out and he grabs the side of Zoe's arm above the elbow and pulls her into his personal space. A locked grip ensures she can't move away or lean back. His face is only a few inches away from her nose. The other girls look on awkwardly as Zoe freezes and her eyes move from side to side, avoiding his intense direct gaze. He then moves on to the girl beside Zoe and does the exact same thing.

A rush of heat burns up my spine as I feel a surge of energy.

Am I seeing this correctly? Is he really doing that?

I try to inhale. Mr Edge, touching me, saying, "gotcha third rib."

I take a big sip of my water bottle.

I feel my feet clench inside my sneakers, and I stand tall, my shadow charming children gathering round my legs.

An inner voice shouts, *'Get your hands off my daughter!'*

It's like my eyes have sliced through the illusion and all that remains is truth and a very clear picture. It's the same fierce instincts that come out of any creature when a mother is protecting her young. A survival intuition programmed into my nervous system mobilises me straightaway to take action.

I don't freeze, laugh or pretend to play along with this game.

I am now forty years old, no longer helpless in a year six classroom.

There is a boundary being crossed here, and I feel it with every fibre of my being. It's the reason why teachers and coaches are required by law to adhere to a code of conduct that states touching children during sport games or in the classroom is wrong. Touching children, period, is not on. Children's intuitive systems and moral compasses are still developing under the age of ten and rely upon mature guidance for protection when they haven't developed the skills to speak up to authority figures. After witnessing the behaviour, I take it on with the team parent coordinator the next day when I see her in the school yard.

"Can we have a meeting about the coach's behaviour? He's touching the girls and being aggressive," I say with a thumping in my chest.

"He's just like an old grandpa," she says. "He doesn't mean any harm. It's because he's a bit deaf. My daughter doesn't mind him touching her."

Advocating for my child means I become her voice, her intuition, her charm. I take a deep breath from my gut and begin to explain how this is a standard not acceptable for our girls. That we can't support it or legally allow it to continue.

The team coordinator takes out a pen and paper and says, "Well, I'll have to record what you're saying because this accusation will be a matter for the police."

The lack of support does not deter me. I feel compassion for those women who can't see truth clearly and are stuck in their own fantasies and delusions. I've been there, too. You need to work through your own fears before you can stand up for others. It's a lot of work.

When I return home, Zoe says, "Mum, I think I want to play netball now."

I withdraw my daughter from the team, effective immediately. A month later, the news hits that the same basketball coach has been disbarred from the sporting organisation for abusing an umpire. I have no emotional reaction. Just a sense of that's about right.

When you first came out of the womb, you took a deep breath. That was the very first intuitive instinct you had to prove to your body that your soul wanted to be here in this form. So, you took a big inhale and breathed your spirit into your lungs. The next thing you did was make a big noise. You screamed a cry and let out a wail. That was your soul authentically expressing itself with its own unique energy. Your voice is a frequency that is created by your soul, and it has its own love language that nobody else is born with. With every act of intuition, your authentic voice gets stronger, and the fearful voice gets weaker. Every act of intuition is a powerful declaration. I am in charge. I get to decide. I am on my side. You can still feel fear without believing it's the truth. Every day is another chance to choose the true me.

What are you doing with your vocal cords?

The unhealed Attached Child is unable to speak up for itself. In the example above, my role as a parent required me to speak on my child's behalf. Often, though, adults don't speak up for themselves when this inner child is activated. The fear of authentic expression is too great a risk. Anytime we feel hesitant or insecure or lost or judgemental, it is our voice and throat chakra that gets suppressed and stores tension. Speaking our truth is easy once we embody our authentic expression. However, we are living in a society that is having an authenticity crisis and a collective throat chakra crisis. We're living for approval from people we don't even know, from people we don't even like or want to spend time with, even from robots on the internet that can predict our emotional reactions.

> According to psychologist Amy Edmonston, we have four basic human needs:
> 1. The need to belong
> 2. The need to learn
> 3. The need to contribute or create
> 4. The need to speak up or express

Number four highlights our innate desire to authentically express who we are at our core, our most natural longing to speak our intuition and to exist without any constriction or masks. We're all masking to some degree so other people can be more comfortable around us.

Patterns of addiction can be traced back to us repressing who we really are. It's so painful to the charming creature that we need to numb and distract it from fully expressing our truth. To authentically express, we need to feel safe to learn, contribute and belong to our values and self-esteem. We are unlearning a whole heap of conditioning, so all these basic human needs are nourished.

But before all those needs are met, we need to know who the hell we are.

Who am I?

We were told as ambitious teenagers that women can have it all. It's no secret that we were told a lie. We can't have it all, but we can *be* it all. In other words, our charming creature isn't outside us as something to seek and capture. It's already inside us and our job is to authentically express it without apologising or shrinking its love for us.

In previous chapters, we've met a bunch of animals which are all unique and living their intuition. These creatures are not confused about the role they play in Noah's Arc kingdom. The mountain goat is not pissed off that it can't fly like an eagle. It's not trying to grow wings because its zone of genius is that it can balance precariously on a cliff edge while being chased by a snow leopard in the high Himalayas. The goat doesn't try to be a bird because it loves being a goat.

A snake doesn't wish to be a donkey. Snakes live for the day they get to shed their skin because no other creature can do this. A snake wakes up and says, *'Today I get to die and leave an old shell behind. How refreshing!'* Why would a snake want to trade in that superpower for fur and long ears? Likewise, a donkey embraces its dharma as the kind of creature that stands in its stoicism. Less likely to startle than a horse, they are proud of their resilience and prefer not to be ridden or raced.

Likewise, creatures not in their natural habitat quickly understand if they're being authentic or not.

When I saw Elizabeth Gilbert speak live in Melbourne in March 2020, it was the month before you-know-what changed the world. She spoke fluidly for two hours as many wise insights poured out: *"The most powerful person in the room is always the most relaxed person."* These words have never left me. To be fully empowered by being comfortable in your own skin, not your pretend scales, is essential to living your intuition.

How can you relax when the skin you are in is not yours? Trying to fit in, rather than belonging to your own charm, is not powerful. An example of this is when I attempted golf lessons so I could play in corporate events and feel like I was part of a team of very important executives doing very important work on the green. I was driven by a fear to meet an aspect of my ego that craved success, superiority and fitting in.

Whenever I tell people this story, they always say, "But that's so not you, Tina."

Standing in the golf shop, I wait nervously for my instructor to appear. Wearing a white polo shirt and neat pants, I feel awkward and self-conscious. It is my fourth lesson and by this stage, it is becoming harder instead of easier to show up.

The instructor comes to meet me and guides me to the easy putting green to go over some basic foundations again.

"No noodle legs," he says. "Straighten your arms. Show me some structure."

I take a giant swing, but end up wobbling all over the place and spinning around on myself.

Eventually, when our six-class package is up, his honest feedback shatters me.

"I can't help you anymore. Your body is not made for golf. You're too bendy. Why don't you try yoga?"

Sometimes our intuition guides us into a crash-and-burn lesson to gain quick clarity. It does this to trick you down a path because it wants you to take a risk and carve your own authentic path.

For me, that risk was leaving my corporate career and the whole package of suits, designer labels, fancy meetings on golf courses and expensive conferences. When I took a leap into the unknown, I found my strength.

To live our intuition is to continue giving up on our ideas of safety and certainty. Intuition is a risk. To live a truly intuitive life, risk may be our most powerful ally. If we can risk living authentically, then perhaps we'll be rewarded with relief. I've never seen anyone take a risk at leaping that is not rewarded a thousand times over. Even if they fail or flounder, the risk has paid off just through the very act of being vulnerable and no longer stagnant.

It takes so much energy to pretend to be something other than ourselves. It also sets us up for failure when we attach our authentic expression to a job, occupation, role, project, ambition or gold medal. Chasing the charm in these things relentlessly leaves us empty in the end.

Maybe you're thinking, *'How can I BE it all then and not burn out in the process?'*

The answer is to *be* comfortable taking risks. To co-create with your intuition, you need to be willing to enter into unfamiliar territory. Being a creative is risky business. Start before you're ready, go for it, feel the fear and dive in anyway. That is the breathless, spine-tingling thrill of it. Exploring our fear as the subject of co-creation is part of the joy of discovering this power instrument which is the charming creature.

The risk when we dive into any ocean is high. We're entering another world full of more creatures than there are on land. It's completely unknown and a much more powerful force than us. Taking risks also means that occasionally there is a real possibility that we will get smashed by waves.

>The project failed.
>Nobody bought my art.
>I burnt the cake.
>I couldn't sell any tickets.
>My partner left me.

When I get guidance from my intuition, often my first response is *'You want me to what! Are you crazy? I don't even know where to start!'*

This is why we often don't get the whole picture in advance, just the breadcrumb or the next actionable step. It's too tempting for fear to paralyse us with a barrage of 'it's too risky' thoughts.

David Bowie said this on how to produce your best work, *"If you feel safe in the area that you're working in, you're not working in the right area. Always go a little further into the water than you feel you're capable of being in. Go a little bit out of your depth, and when you don't feel that your feet are quite touching the bottom, you're just about in the right place to do something exciting."*

> "When your self-worth isn't on the line, it becomes easier to take risks. You get more of what you want because you're more willing to risk trying."
> —Katherine Morgan Schafler

Dare to take risks and flex your intuition like a muscle. If it's uncomfortable, it's working.

When we make ourselves available for the inflow of creative energy, we accept not only her generative power but also her ability to destroy whatever stands in the way of our full aliveness. The fierce Goddess Kali, the devourer of all things, is the consort of the Hindu God of the Himalaya, Holy Shiva the destroyer. There is no transformation without breakdown, death, rebirth and risk. There's always another layer to peel, another skin to shed, another evolution revealing a deeper version of ourselves. We can always go too fast, but we can never go too deep in our lives. One way to avoid the discomfort of change is to skim fast over the surface. Depth, on the other hand, is why we are here in human form. To risk everything by being willing to know who we are at our very core. Raw and risky.

Intuition is understanding the immutability of your worth. You don't doubt your hunches because you know you can count on yourself in moments of uncertainty. You're more willing to fall and fail because you've already won. It cannot be risky when you esteem yourself just for existing. There is nothing you need to do or control or prove.

Evolution demands we take risks and forget tradition because intuition will always lead us into the unknown. Doing the same thing and staying in the familiar safe zone can be a result of ignoring our intuition and letting the past inform our choices. We are continually being asked to move away from 'always' and towards 'new'. Evolving is, in essence, not so much a practice as it is the entire force of our deepest nature, our primal need, to develop self-realisation. It is this impulse and longing towards our intuition that is the persistent beckoning ache which will not leave us alone.

What does your next leap of faith look like? Do the thing that scares you the most.

Author Bronnie May, discussing the number one regret of the dying, writes as number one, *"I wish I had the courage to live a life true to myself."*

May we all start to have the courage to be ourselves.

What does your next leap of faith look like? Do the thing that scares you the most.

I am nine years old, and at a family backyard barbeque. There are grandparents, cousins, uncles, aunties, great uncles and aunties and neighbours all gathering in the garden.

"C'mon," I say to my cousins and sister. "Let's practise!"

We're rehearsing a show to perform for the grown-ups. I love acting and creating dances at these events. It's so much fun to be a character and make up stories and plays. I'm preparing for my role as a perfect and pompous butler. With prop in hand, I practise my lines and walk around the room, balancing the plate with a tea towel thrown over my arm.

"Look at me. I'm so professional," I yell out.

The time comes to present to our captive audience. I walk onto the 'stage' and the ceramic dish slips off my fingers and smashes into pieces on the concrete.

The plate cracks around my feet. I forget my next line.

"Uhhhhh, ummm," My body freezes like a statue. I run away to my room and hide. I dive into bed and throw the doona cover over my head, trying to disappear. Nobody will see me. My invisible wounded child is safe.

I hear a voice.

"Tina, Tina, it's aunty Gwen."

Sniff sniff, I try to stay quiet under the covers as I feel her sit on the bed beside me.

"You know, only the smartest people choke and drop things," she says.

"You are one of the brave ones that has a go. The audience doesn't get to be brave."

Slowly, I peek out from smothering myself and take a gasp of air.

Gwen gently pats my belly and says, "I bet if you go back out there, chin up, chest out, you will get to be brave again, and we'll get to clap at your courageous voice."

"Where's my tea towel?" I ask.

"That's the girl. Go on," she encourages, and takes me by the hand to the backyard.

I feel her warm palm in mine and know everything will be ok.

Sometimes, I open my mouth to roar like a lion, and deliver instead the tiny peep of a mouse. Which charming creature is inside me? Perhaps this mouse is just courage with smaller paws. Poet David Whyte describes this as courageous speech, *"Because no matter what we say, we are revealed as the voice emerges literally from the body as a representation of our inner world."* The fear of authentic expression lives in the energy centre of the throat chakra and can surface when we find ourselves emerging out of a cocoon in a new, unfamiliar form. It's a fear that rises especially when we're being creative or innovative. I'll remind 'little tina' that *the world really has no use for your broken shame. It craves your playfulness, charm and knowledge.*

In 2018, when I was in Bali, I got my first tattoo. I was sober. It marked the end of a retreat where I was full on spirit and natural endorphins. The ink is black and spells out the word love within an infinity symbol. It's so small on the side of my left foot my forty-four-year-old eyes need glasses now to read it.

I will regret the true thing I didn't say for the rest of my life.

"Make it bigger."

At the time, I was watching the artist work away and wanted to say, "Make it bigger."

Squinting while reading the word 'love' felt effortful and like hard work. Is this sacred tattoo going to contribute to my crow's feet or help fire up my rebellious charm?

I wanted love like flashing neon in a giant sign so love couldn't miss me. Instead of speaking my truth, I stayed silent and ignored my charming creature who was dancing around inside, shouting for me to show more charm.

"Don't play small or hide like a huntsman spider. Wear your art on the outside and be bold."

Instead, the rogue woman's voice overpowered, "Keep it tiny. You don't want to upset your family or be a terrible role model for your children. What will people think? Don't make others uncomfortable by changing too fast. This is a huge mistake."

This time, the voice of fear had its own way and I stayed small, but I was mighty. I walked out of my hotel as I breathed in a final waft of Balinese smog and headed towards the airport.

Sometimes, one small peep for a woman is a giant roar for womankind.

Kitsugi is the restorative Japanese art of repairing broken ceramics with gold. The resulting piece is considered more beautiful. We all have our scars, old patterns or samskaras. On the days when we feel ashamed of our scars, our thoughts descend to ugliness rather than the beauty that we survived one hundred percent of our humiliating days. I personally wouldn't be leading retreats today if it weren't for my deep longing to transform wounds into wisdom or smashed plates into gold. There is a whole art form devoted to this practice.

The many powerful messages *kintsugi* conveys:
1. Breakages in our hearts and souls are inevitable.
2. We are more resilient than we think.
3. Imperfection is interesting.
4. We can grow from traumatic loss, grief and suffering, which shape our values and give our lives meaning.
5. Intuition knows how to mend.

"The world breaks everyone and afterward many are strong at the broken places."
—Ernest Hemingway

PRACTICE BREATHWORK

WOODCHOPPER'S BREATH

WHAT IS ITS CHARM?

This practice clears the throat chakra for the purpose of authentic expression. What we suppress most are difficult emotions such as anger and rage. Trying to shut them down can be problematic and have very damaging effects on our health. Swallowing our feelings by trying to be 'good girls' or calm spiritual people does not help our intuition. Eventually, we become angry at being angry and the heat within builds and finds its way out in unhelpful and harmful ways. The question to ask yourself is, *'Would you rather the pain of expressing yourself and not being accepted, or not expressing yourself and being accepted?'* Goddess Kali encourages authenticity over rejection any day. She activates fierceness through using her tongue and voice as a tool to release fear. Its charm is in making a lot of noise and letting go of pent-up frustration.

THE TYPE OF FEAR IT LOVES
Fear of authentic expression.

HOW TO DO IT?

1. Think of something that annoys you in your life. Start with these word prompts:
   - I'm so angry at ...
   - I'm so angry because ...
   - I'm so angry I want to ...

Once you've said aloud what you're angry at:

2. Stand straight with your legs wide apart and your shoulders squared.
3. Take Kali mudra with your hands and raise them above your head as if holding a wood chopping axe.
4. Breathe in and, while exhaling, bend down with full force as if you are chopping wood. Exaggerate the exhale, making a 'HA' sound that is typical of doing hard work to flush it all out.
5. Let your arms swing down between your legs when you bend down.
6. Raise yourself to standing and repeat again up to twenty times.

Really give yourself over to it.

JOURNAL PROMPTS

1. Why don't I act on my intuition?
2. How does being a 'good girl' interfere with me asking for what I want?
3. Why do I fear empowering others?
4. Why do I sabotage my own choices?

Medusa

CHAPTER 12

MEDUSA JELLYFISH

Chakra:	Third Eye [Ajna]
Consciousness:	Divine
Mantra:	Hummmmm
Location:	Brain, eyes, ears, nose, pituitary/pineal gland
Element:	Subtle intelligence
Challenge:	Fear of seeing the truth, seeing through mental illusions
Power:	Discernment, intuitive knowledge, emotional intelligence
Breath:	Brahmari (Bee Breath) Pranayama

"Exploring is an attitude, really, a quality of attention to the world around you. Exploration demands a refusal of all the usual maps; of the world, of how you're told to live your one and only life."

—Kate Harris

"Ahh, grazie," I say, as they place a blue and white patterned bowl in front of me full of steaming fresh calamari, prawns and fish.

"Oh, may I also have some parmigiano cheese?" I ask the waiter who looks at me in horror.

He lifts his arms up and gestures like he's talking through the palms of his hands.

"Noh!" he yells at me unapologetically. "Noh fromage on seafood."

I have just committed a sin, an Italian 'faux pas'. Fish and cheese are not friends. Of course, it makes complete sense—why would farmed dairy even get a look in compared to such oceanic freshness?

When it comes to food, certain customs are highly spiritful. When a food is full of energy and vigour, it is charming all on its own. Messing with it is a giant risk.

I nod my head in respect and begin twirling the long strands around my fork, accepting that God is in the pasta perfectly as it stands. If you ask any of my family or close friends what my last meal request on earth would be, they would answer with no hesitation. Seafood pasta. If 'tutti de mare' is on a menu, even in a Chinese restaurant, I'll order it. It makes sense that I would be drawn to its origin circled on a map on this Sicilian island at the end of the boot, a dish filled with charming creatures from the mysterious otherworldly ocean.

Perhaps it is my longing to be as close as possible to the mystery of their sea home. The flavours of fish and crustaceans mix through the long strands of linguini, all swimming in a broth that contains depth and zest. Perhaps it's about the person behind the catch. The lone Italian fisherman down by the dock, cigarette hanging out the corner of his lips, handing over a bag of gleaming clicking mussels in exchange for ten euros. The story behind this meal connects me in a strange way with the salt water inside my own cells. I am here with no other agenda other than to look forwards to my next meal and float in the majestic, emerald Mediterranean. The best holidays always have this sense of drifting aimlessly with no ambition, a proper cure. A pleasure cure.

After my last mouthful, I get up from the table and announce to my family that I'm going for a swim. I'm bursting to get wet and experience that first dive into the body of water that has been teasing me through lunch. I leave the restaurant, grabbing a towel by the side of the pool, and walk towards the waves crashing against the rocks. My pale white complexion stands out amongst the crowd of tanned beach goers. I strip off my kaftan, tip-toeing across the pebbles and rocks as fast as I can. With such unstable moving ground beneath my feet, I struggle to keep my balance with flailing waving arms acting as rudders through space. I find my way to the shore and grasp onto a boulder to catch my breath.

Three small girls about age six or seven play in front of me with long pink braids woven through their mermaid holiday hair. Their little voices yelling, "Noh!" and laughing in Italian make me smile. Yes, I could pretend to be a mermaid too, in this fantastical moment. I walk into the water and imagine briefly that my long, jet-lagged legs are a glamorous sleek tail. I dive headfirst into the water. Feeling the rush of cold waves wash over me, the stress and fatigue dissolve. I let the weight of my bones gently bring me back up to the surface without forcing or rushing. My head pops up and I look around in disbelief back at the coastline with the horizon behind me. A thousand colourful umbrellas line the shore and I exhale out a sigh of relief to be baptised at last by 'The Med'. Suddenly, I'm jolted violently out of my sublime suspension as something sharp stings the side of my torso.

"Arghhhh!" I yell, turning my head to see what it is. A second attack on my left shoulder.

"Faaaark!" Now I know exactly what my nervous system has just communicated to my brain. *Get out of the water right now.*

I start to move my arms and swim like a crazy octopus to the shore. Shit, I've been done by a jellyfish. The throbbing increases and the sting intensifies as I pull myself out of the ocean and exit the scene. To anyone observing, they might mistakenly see a middle-aged, drunken Aussie stumbling and swearing while clutching her chest inappropriately. This strategy gains attention as two Italian lifeguards attentively come to my rescue, waving one hand in the air and carrying a tube of cream in the other.

"Si, Si. Medusa, Medusa!"

Who is Medusa, I think to myself for a split second before yelling out, "I've been stung."

The lifeguards give me the same look as the disapproving waiter and begin to apply lotion straight onto my skin. I know this look. It is the same look the taxi driver gave me on the way here from the airport while offering some crucial advice ...

"Almond milk kills the coffee."

"Ice cubes in wine is a sin."

"Noh fromage on seafood!!!"

And the really obvious sign stuck on a post at the water's edge ...

"DANGER. MEDUSA JELLYFISH.
DO NOT SWIM IN OCEAN."

Somewhere off the coast of Sicily, I am kissed by a jellyfish. In the land of love, it wrapped its romantic tentacles around the left side of my heart, flaring up an old, injured nerve just to remind me of the tortured pain one must endure to appreciate real pleasure. It was a strange kind of blessing from this charming creature known as Medusa that doesn't have a brain or heart, just a nervous system. I can relate to its simple form, often just feeling like a bunch of nerves floating in a body of subconscious soup.

Ouch, but a million 'thank you's for waking up my charm.

In his article, *"Medusa: Cruel Monster or Misunderstood Victim. The Tragic Story of One of the Most Notorious Rapes in Greek Mythology"* Nick Iakovidis writes, *"By the time of early Archaic Greece (800-600 BCE) Medusa was already a very popular figure but very misunderstood. She was brutally raped by Poseidon in the Temple of Athena and was then cursed to transform into a hideous monster, who petrified its victims with one gaze of her eyes."*

Medusa was the main antagonist of Perseus, who eventually managed to kill her by brutally severing her head from its body. These mythologies can teach us so much about our archetypal patterns. According to the myth, it was Goddess Athena who then turned Medusa's hair into snakes as punishment. This patriarchal narrative pitted women against each other and communicated that if a woman was raped, it was the woman's fault.

Most would recognise Medusa. The Greek Goddess has live snakes on her head instead of hair, the upper body of a woman, the lower body of a serpent and eyes that could turn any man into stone just by one look.

Her face is the perfect representation of the duality of nature. Monster and woman, good and evil, beauty and ugliness, victim and villain, Medusa's head gathers all the above contradicting opposites into a single creature. It is quite interesting to notice that for the ancient Greek male-leading societies, female beauty was often associated with great danger, and therefore it was seen as necessary to be isolated or exterminated from the world.

Medusa's myth, on which she acquired both a monstrous and a human side, was an attempt by the patriarchal powers to dehumanise women and connect the female gender with monstrous un-charming elements, destroying any charm that could be perceived as powerful.

And that is the big little traumatic story we were taught of Medusa as kids. An infamous, not-so-charming creature to be feared, otherwise known as the Snake Goddess or Monster Head.

Medusa since has become a symbol for oppressed and abused

women around the world. Her towering seven-foot statue stands outside the criminal courthouse in lower Manhattan across the street from where men accused of sexual assault during the 'Me Too' movement were prosecuted, including Harvey Weinstein. She stands with a sword in her left hand and the severed head of Perseus dangling from her right hand. This is a reversal of the original myth which tells of Perseus slaying Medusa and using her head as a weapon to turn people to stone with her scary stare.

Changing this narrative from chilling cruelty to charm is where the power lies. Where domestic abuse and sexual crimes against women are unfortunately still common, stories like this need to be retold through a soul lense so we can educate one another and change the paradigm. It is through the sixth chakra and the powerful energy centre of seeing only truth that all illusions are sliced away with practised discernment.

Our children would do better if we role-modelled Medusas instead of Little Mermaid Princesses powerless to walk on their own two legs until kissed by a prince.

> "The moment a woman gives birth to her baby, she also gives birth to her own medicine. Her Intuition."

That was the opening sentence I wrote in my first memoir, *"Mother's Medicine"*. Within my experience of becoming a mother, it was true that I found my power. But now that I know better, I see it has a much broader context. The next paragraph of my first memoir was more accurate ... *"Contrary to what many people believe, intuition is not a gift—it is programmed in all of us."* Intuition is *not* just reserved for mothers or women and is naturally born with our first breath. As Albert Einstein wrote, *"The intuitive mind is a sacred gift and the *rational mind is a faithful servant. We have created a society that honours the servant and has forgotten the gift."*

I'm going to be bold and disagree with Einstein. He was a smart dude, but he was wrong. Intuition is not a gift. Contrary to what you hear, it's not special, it's not a superpower, it's not found in the hippy shops, the oracle cards, the sage, the crystals, the psychics or in your third eye. Reducing intuition to spiritual entertainment, material to be bought, or even worse, 'women's intuition' has done both men and women a disservice by keeping it in the domestic home, or reserved for maternal instinct or secret witchy woo-woo circles.

How many people have had the experience of thinking about somebody and one second later the phone rings or texts and it is them? This is the scientific term for quantum entanglement called non-local intuition, or to quote Einstein again, *"spooky action at a distance"*. It supports the idea that we create our own reality, or that mental creation precedes physical creation. We have to have a thought or receive the information before we can manifest it into form. Intuition is every human being's natural state that we were born knowing. However, we're not trained to see ourselves as an instrument of *power*.

'Women's intuition' was a term used to label 'hypersensitive' women and give men ownership over the rational and logical mind. These stereotypes tend to flatten and divide us as a culture, and while this is not a debate over gender intelligence, it is a reminder that we carry both energies and our minds are fluid. In a male-dominant world, it can be challenging to stay in our feminine nature. In business, we are used to the male paradigm of leadership, where everyone operates from their left brain of logic, analytics and control, subsequently ignoring the right side, which is creative, connecting and imaginative.

In a patriarchy, people lead from the left where knowledge is limited by physical evidence and disregards how we know something without knowing how we know it. When we find ourselves over explaining our choices in front of others, it sends the message to our intuition that we are not enough on our own.

Einstein was correct in saying that when both minds work together in the right relationship with each other, for example, when our head serves our heart, we can lead with our values and express our authentic selves. Without this moral compass, the human brain will justify any decision. Intuition is our investment in living a moral life and expressing kindness to others, our capacity for awe and wonder, and our receptivity to beauty. We notice this when we spend time in nature. It nurtures and delights this part of our imaginative mind. Together, both minds are partners. However, in order to break down the binary, we must open ourselves up to discernment. The world needs more courageous imagination, but instead, it's getting a lot of mental noise, distraction and confusion.

How do you know the difference between intuition and wishful thinking, illusion, or mental noise? There are some decisions in life that are simply too big for your mind to make. When we mix up the messages from the mind with the messages from our intuition, it can result in some very painful outcomes. The mental body is a different frequency to intuitive consciousness. At the level of the sixth chakra, we start to refine the difference between what is monkey-mind, useless guidance and what is true-blue intuition. The mind spins off into familiar fantasy and projection, which is a comfortable place for the ego. The difference is intuition makes you uncomfortable and fantasy does not.

Our power to face fear and find safety within lies in our ability to discern. Discernment is the power through which we co-create the quality of our lives. The familiar feels safe, but it's not always healthy or taking us in the direction of our dreams.

I've heard all the wellness hacks and quick fixes out there that promise to make this fear-facing process easier, including crazy apple cider vinegar cleanses and hot coal fire walking. What makes us unique as a species compared to other charming creatures, such as birds, bees and trees, is that we have the ability to discern and choose. Choice puts us in a unique position. It means we have options. The option to empower ourselves or disempower ourselves.

How can you know whether it's fear versus intuition?

Choosing from intuition is empowering, whereas choosing from fear is not.

Often, we create chaos the moment truth or power comes too close to us. We sometimes self-sabotage if we are unwilling to hear the truth. Choosing to become more powerful comes with responsibility, and that is what frightens us the most.

What will this choice cost me in terms of my power?

Am I afraid of the responsibility that comes with being a powerful woman?

Will this choice empower me, or will it disempower me?

We have the power to choose and we're always one decision away from a completely different life. When it comes to our health, it's actually the smallest decisions that have the most power, the ones we make when nobody is watching. Be a change maker. All our human suffering is caused by resistance to change. Resistance to where our intuition wants to guide us.

What must we accept or let go of in order for life to reveal its song to us? Whether it is by choice or not, letting go of past patterns allows room for the unexpected and miraculous to enter. Radical taking away of something seemingly solid and foundational is an archetypal pattern of power that moves through us. The unlocking of our intuitive energy has a great impact on our life because it is a soul rebirth. Once we take everything away that is false, all that remains is our true nature. Sometimes you need to let go. Sometimes you need to go all in. It all boils down to making the risky decision.

How to make a discerning decision
1. Remove all outside influencers and distractions.
2. Be careful of the counsel you choose. E.g., that person's role is not to give advice but to simply listen so you can hear yourself speak out loud.
3. Get still and feel inside. Intuition will speak through your body.
4. The decision will be a knowing without any drama, justifications or stories attached to it.
5. The decision won't make sense to your rational mind or to others who are close to you.
6. Your intuition won't reveal the whole picture, just the next step.
7. When you're ready to decide, expect fear. Your heart will pound, and your hands will shake. That's normal, so accept it will be very uncomfortable.
8. As soon as the decision is made, be prepared for the light to return!

·········· **PRACTICE BREATHWORK** ··········

BRAHMARI BEE BREATH

WHAT IS ITS CHARM?

Brahmari is a pranayama technique which derives its name from the black Indian bee called Bhramari. Its charm is its effectiveness at instantly calming down the mind. If you have particularly busy thoughts or are in an anxious mental loop, this breath can be a circuit breaker. Also, it's a useful starting point for those who are 'too busy' to meditate. Essentially, you make a humming sound like a bee. The vibration clears the energy centre of the sixth chakra behind the eyes. When we are cloudy or foggy in the brain, we can't discern the truth. Decisions become confusing and anxiety increases. The bee is considered a symbolic charming creature of miracles and spirituality, and when harnessed intentionally, will slow down racing thoughts and make space for magic!

THE TYPE OF FEAR IT LOVES
Fear of seeing the truth.

HOW DO I DO IT?

1. Sit up comfortably, with your back straight and close your eyes.
2. Inhale deeply through your nose. Exhale through your nose while making a 'mmmmm' humming sound, just like a buzzing bee.
3. Experiment with different pitches and see the different effects.
4. Option to use the traditional Shanmukhi mudra: place your hands on either side of your face with one thumb covering each ear, the index fingers lightly touching your eyelids, the middle fingers on the side of your nose, the ring fingers above your lips, and the pinkie fingers just below.
5. Repeat six to eight times.

JOURNAL PROMPTS

1. What is illusion in my life and what is true clear power?
2. Who has been my darkest teacher?

A discerning choice feels in my body like ...
And finally, the wisest choice I've ever made is ...

Bhuvaneshwari

CHAPTER 13

DON'T DIE TRYING

Chakra: Crown [Sahasrar]
Consciousness: Union
Mantra: Om Shrim Hrim Shrim Bhuvaneshwarayei Namaha
Location: Top of the head, skin, muscular system, skeletal system
Element: Consciousness
Challenge: Fear of death, spiritual abandonment, 'dark night of the soul'
Power: Cosmic mother, prayer, mystical presence, faith
Breath: 4/7/8 Breath Retention Pranayama

I pray you'll be our eyes, and watch us where we go
And help us to be wise in times when we don't know
Let this be our prayer, when we lose our way
Lead us to a place, guide us with your grace
To a place where we'll be safe.
—"The Prayer" [Verse quoted by Anthony Callea]

"Don't try too hard," Nan says with a wink, as she pats the back of the doctor's hand from the side of her bed. A cardiologist is preparing some medicine to reduce the risk of further coronary events.

"Don't try too hard. I'm tired," she says again.

Inside a body that is ready to die, trying is lying. Nan is one hundred and one years old and on 8 May 2019, is taken to a Brisbane hospital by ambulance after having a heart attack at home. It is the same day I launch my first book, *"Mother's Medicine"*, and I'm preparing for an evening event to celebrate with family and friends. My mum, noticeably absent, is holding vigil by her mother's bedside in Brisbane.

I slip the gold, sparkly dress over my head and look in the full-length mirror.

Inhale, I twirl.

Exhale, I smile.

I hardly ever wear a dress, so I pace around my room, rehearsing what I'll say, thrilled not to be in tight activewear. At 5.00 pm, the phone rings and I answer straightaway while doing my makeup. Mum's name flashes on my phone.

"Hi Tina."

There's a long silence and I don't try to fill it.

"Nan has just passed away."

I hear the empty, hollow grief in mum's voice, and I nod silently.

"I know you're about to go to your book launch but thought you'd want to know," she says.

"I don't know what to say," I stammer.

I hug her through the phone and tell her I'll call her the next day.

Collapsing on my bedroom floor, I stare at the wall. Mixed with adrenalin is now shock. But then it makes sense. Nan's spiritful humour. Well, of course, she is dead. She wants to be at this important moment in my life, so her soul just decided to depart her old body as soon as possible.

Nan's flying to Melbourne!

Birth and death in the same day. I am feeling sadness and the joy of life simultaneously.

I remember Nan's favourite song, *"The Prayer"*, and press play on Spotify while beginning to hum. It's not the original version by Italian opera singer, Andrea Bocelli, but by her preferred beloved Aussie, Anthony Callea.

"Guide us with your grace, to a place where we'll be safe."

Isn't that all we can really ask for in the end?

I ask Nan for courage, take a huge breath, strap on my high heels, and let my charm lead as I walk down the stairs.

Prayer is communing with our charming creature. It aligns the root of us to our crown chakra and infuses us again with the knowing that we are both human and divine. Prayer can feel like a personalised love letter to our hearts while at the same time being so enlarged and universal it has nothing to do with our ego's wants and needs.

Mantra, or repeated prayer, is taught in most meditation and yoga schools. The conscious repetition gives the mind something to chew on which is like an intentional distraction. The sound technology of mantra is also extremely powerful when invoking the goddess archetypes. The vibrations stimulate energetic channels on the roof of your mouth, sending specific signals to your brain. Like a radio antenna, the Universe picks up on these signals and brings you into alignment with the archetypal patterns.

Prayer can be both a science and an art with our body as the instrument, a vibratory vessel. Prayer heals us, especially when it's combined with slow and mindful breathing. In chapter ten, we were introduced to the Buddhist mantra *Om Mani Padme Hum*. Each chanted line takes six seconds to inhale before the next round begins again, which consequently slows down the breath.

In James Nestor's book, *"Breath"*, his research showed, *"the most efficient breathing rhythm occurred when both the length of respirations and total breaths per minute were locked into a spooky symmetry: 5.5 second inhales followed by 5.5 second exhales, which works out almost exactly to 5.5 breaths per minute. This was the same pattern of the rosary and Catholic chanting cycle of Ave Maria. Other cultural traditions across many countries all use similar prayer techniques of slow breathing."*

As you travel with your spirit to mantrafy your breath throughout each day, you'll start to feel your whole being as a walking prayer instead of unconsciously indulging your habitual mental chatter. We need this level of help to get beyond ourselves. To get beyond the beyond. If we don't ask for guidance from our intuition or the goddesses, don't expect to get answers.

There are some things we just can't do on our own, inside our own rational minds.

What's the difference between me praying and me nattering to myself in my head?

Pray and you shall receive an instruction, a sign, a nudge. Natter in your head and you become caught up in drama and desires.

When we're nattering, we don't tend to ask questions such as:
- Please help me find the strength to get through this. *A high-vibration ask.*
- Give me the courage to be authentic. *A brave demand.*
- Increase my capacity to forgive? *A humble request.*
- Help me love those I find difficult to love. *A sacred challenge.*

Prayer is asking grace to leave you better than how it found you, which is more conversational. It engages the charming creature in an intimate way.

This prayer is not the same as nattering.

Nattering sounds more like:
- I want more money.
- Get me a better job.
- Help me lose weight.
- Show me where I left my keys.

Perhaps the most popular of all prayers, across all cultures and languages, is that for world peace. Peace is not just given to us. It's something we need to practise. We begin by cultivating our own sense of inner peace first, so it can ripple out to others. To stop the war within ourselves takes every bit of courageous charm we possess. When we engage in conflict or harshly judge or criticise ourselves, we are regressing into a past pattern instead of seeking an alternative. It is our responsibility as charming creatures to imagine and create a new future, not to relive and rehash the past.

Every spiritual tradition uses prayer and guides us out of violence and towards a higher place. It is beyond religion to pray because we're wired to communicate with an energy greater than us, not a doctrine or set of stiff beliefs.

Help from the higher realms is holy. Clarissa Pinkola Estes writes, *"If you cannot make something better or different, then make it holy."* On a planet where fixing what is severely broken seems so out of reach, we can at least make the moment holy through prayer. Turning your life into a living prayer and act of devotion makes space for grace.

On a small scale, this might be, *do I yell at my child or not? Can I just let it be? Can I accept her choices?*

Prayer is a necessary action to reach forgiveness. It doesn't make sense to our judging brain to forgive someone who did the wrong thing. We need prayer to move past the paradox of good and bad, or right and wrong. Help is holy, and it is also mystical. Most of us try initially to forgive with our minds, only to find that we stay in trying mode. *I'm trying to forgive* becomes our story. Trying is lying. What we really mean is *'I'm still so vengeful I can't release the fantasy of wanting to hurt that person.'* In order to truly forgive, we need to go through an ego death to transcend that fear. It requires praying for courage and compassion to go through a somatic process and letting the warring part of your body die. There are consequences to committing to a prayer life.

Examined more closely:
- You can't hold on to resentments or grudges.
- You need to empower other people.
- You need to forgive yourself and let go of self-loathing.
- You need to stop the war within.
- You can no longer let your wounds define you.
- You can't be a victim of anything because blaming others is not an option.
- You have to choose integrity over comfort.
- You need to initiate difficult conversations to dissolve tension in relationships.
- Your addictions can no longer control you.
- You say 'yes' to your intuition even when it pisses people off who love you.

It's a big ask from the Universe.

What if you don't want to be this empowered?

There will be some days on the 'life plane' when we are leading from the front as the pilot, and other days when we are unconsciously being dragged from the back with all the other passengers. Some seasons, we're laying down future flight plans and other times, autopilot determines our destined path!

I don't recall ever telling anybody this. It's one of those secrets from your youth that you forget about and then a memory pops back into your consciousness and you start to join all the dots of your life. When I was nineteen years old, I decided I wanted to be a pilot and fly aeroplanes. I researched the two major airline schools, Qantas and

Ansett at the time, to understand what it would take to train for and obtain a qualified commercial license.

There was something about flying up high into spaciousness that attracted me to defying gravity. While asleep, I often dreamed of flying through the air, floating into space and being all bird-like and free spirited. It never occurred to me that a young woman couldn't do this within a male-dominated profession, so I persisted.

Reading more about the ins and outs of becoming a pilot, my dreams were crushed when I realised it was going to cost me in excess of one hundred thousand dollars. On top of that, not having studied physics as a broad science subject would severely limit the application process.

Determined, I started going down the path of how I could fly for free. The answer? Join the army! If the government pays for my qualification, I'll serve my country. I went as far as going to a public Open Day for the Brisbane Army Reserves and sitting down for an interview with a very official-looking man in an Air Force uniform. I looked like their ideal recruit. Wearing flip-flops, harem pants and fiddling with my newly pierced nose stud, I sat down, took a big breath and then blurted, "I want to be a pilot."

Within about five minutes, the energy in the room crashed around me and I sensed my muscles contract and my heart deflate. The amount of 'yes, sir', 'no, sir' and the list of rules and regulations a military life demanded drained my spirits faster than cancelling Christmas. An Aquarian woman being told what to do and obeying commands in the Air Force was going to be a challenge. I didn't have the maverick motivation, nor did I want to go to war.

I know travel and airports are written into my soul contract somehow, but I'd need to find another way to soar. The responsibility of the charming creature is to imagine and commit to creating this new future. It is not the goal to be perfect at it. We're going to fumble and fall many times. However, pray and the sky will open up to endless possibilities.

"It matters not how far you go, what matters is how alive you are."
—Paul Theroux

My Nan lived to be a centurion, a warrior of aging. In fact, her name, Nina, in its Native American origin means 'mighty' and she absolutely refused to be put into a nursing home. Of course, she was scared of lots of other things, like her grandchildren travelling and participating in 'unsafe', life-threatening activities such as skiing, surfing and public speaking. But physically, she was like Mighty Mouse. A superhero spiritful creature, she faced many traumas in her life with grace and flow. She kept her breast cancer a carefree secret during her final decade until surrendering to mastectomy surgery at age ninety-nine when the tumour naturally ulcerated through her skin.

Any of us could die any day of any number of causes, and we are none the wiser to the who, when and how it will happen. This is the wonderful mystery of our existence, and at times, the fear that gives life its meaning. Everything I love will be let go of, and there is nothing I can do to avoid this. I will let go of my favourite places, sights, sounds, smells, core beliefs and people. Finally, I must let go of my body. I can't take my body with me, and neither can you. That makes us the same. We are both vulnerable to a life that is not guaranteed. In essence, embracing this *is* the spiritful journey. The spiritful journey is not linear, it's not a competition, and it's not a race.

Since the pandemic, I've sought out therapy and asked for help in new places I previously didn't need. I think every single one of us is still processing trauma from the last few years, whether we're conscious of it or not. I've had to challenge old patterns and core beliefs and face a lot of sadness around how hard I can be on myself. Our habits and heartaches will always be part of our story, but they will never be the *end* to our story.

That eight-year-old girl who clings so desperately to the clipboard of control is slowly learning she is safe in the arms of a forty-four-year-old wise woman. You have goddesses and guides and invisible creatures that are with you, watching over your destiny. Yes, it's extremely daunting at times, and will demand so much from you. And yet, you're on the right, authentic path for your soul's dreams to come true. Powerful prayer sounds like the words my seven-year-old daughter read out at Nan's funeral.

> *Dear GG,*
> *I hope you have a good life in heaven.*
> *I love you so much because you are thoughtful and have a really kind heart.*
> *I wonder if you are going to have a spirit animal?*
> *And if you do have a spirit animal, I think a Manta-ray would really suit you. Because they are graceful and elegant like you.*
> *From your great-grandchild, Zoë*

In the end, we all pray to become our spiritful animals, charming our way through 'heaven' or the beyond. You ask the charming creature to take you where you need to go. You pray with devotion and dedication, and here is the reply. Don't try too hard. Just be yourself.

"Every woman has a vocation to become someone: but she must understand clearly that in order to fulfil her vocation she can only be one person: herself."
—Thomas Merton

One of my devoted students, Dr George Halasz, a Psychiatrist and former Senior Lecturer at Monash University, wrote the following prayer after a breathwork class.

I held my breath
I held my death

I inhaled my breath
I exhaled my death

I breathed into my body
I breathed into my breath
I reclaimed my body
I reclaimed my breath

I connect with my farewell
I breathe from breath to breath

He described the experience, "If you have experienced hitting the proverbial brick wall, felt overwhelmed with stress or simply exhausted your energy, I can suggest an idea that may sound familiar but it is a very different approach- take a deep dive into your breath. I suggest Tina Bruce's breathing class to open inner doors to vitality, I found the experience essential to restore a balance I had lost. Guided by her intuition blended with serious evidence based awareness I found the results deeply grounding and encouraging ... you may also."

This is a prayer I wrote using the journal prompt, *'I am truly feeling.'*

PRAYER: I AM TRULY FEELING

I am truly feeling grateful for the world turning. Life goes on as I go in. I see that growth and death and birth are a tapestry of movement and I can be still in the middle.

I am truly feeling that I am passing through people and places like a leaf in the wind.

I touch some and avoid others.

I am truly feeling when I stop and slow down inside the eye of the hurricane.

I am truly feeling a longing to help, but not knowing how.

I am truly feeling that my existence is about baring this rawness.

I am truly feeling that living by your own rules and giving from this place is the key to charm.

I am truly feeling that grasping onto someone else's life will not go so well.

I am truly feeling that rejection hurts and I can't control it. If it's not personal, then why does it hurt?

I am truly feeling that I can't drag my old life around with me.

I am truly feeling everything is ok when we know we're not alone in our experience.

I am truly feeling it's time to bow to what beckons.

PRACTICE BREATHWORK

4/7/8 BREATH

WHAT IS ITS CHARM?

The 4/7/8 breathwork is based on a pranayama technique and was developed by Dr Andrew Weil. It is described as a natural tranquiliser for the nervous system. So much of our life has to do with learning how to live under pressure, of balancing responsibilities and trying to create space in which to catch our breath. Spaciousness is like a soothing balm for the parasympathetic nervous system. It's not just a place we go. It's where we come from. There's a remembrance of our soul and its infinite nature. Space promotes less stress and this pranayama technique has a natural calming effect. Its charm is that it can invoke the sensation of flying or floating out of heaviness. It lifts us up towards the light and makes room for possibility. It opens up the crown chakra and strengthens our connection to spiritual dimensions beyond this one human life. As we suspend our breath, we automatically release the fear of death by creating this still point for our mind and body. Bhuvaneshwari is the supreme Goddess of infinite space who can hold both of these opposites. She supports the pause in between each breath and its retention at the top of the inhale as an acceptance of life and death, or of physical form and the subtle body. This breath pattern helps you dissolve fear and awaken your intuition. The opposite of death is breath. Is there life after death? Breathe and see.

THE TYPE OF FEAR IT LOVES
Fear of death.

HOW DO I DO IT?

1. Find a comfortable seat and put the tip of your tongue behind your upper front teeth.
2. Close your eyes and take a deep breath in through your nose for the count of four.
3. Hold your breath for the count of seven and observe the space.
4. Exhale completely through your mouth for the count of eight, make a whoosh sound, observe the space as your lungs are empty. Note: always inhale quietly through your nose, exhale audibly through your mouth.
5. Now inhale again and repeat the cycle four more times for a total of five breaths.

JOURNAL PROMPTS

1. How does my charming creature pray?
2. What goddesses are travelling with me?
3. What is a wild dream that I've never told anyone?
4. What does living my Intuitive Mountain mean to me?

The Day We Die by Southern Bushmen

The day we die
the wind comes down
to take away
our footprints.

The wind makes dust
to cover up
the marks we left
while walking.

For otherwise
the thing would seem
as if we were
still living.

Therefore the wind
is he who comes
to blow away
our footprints.

EPILOGUE

I turned to my community and asked them *what does living your Intuitive Mountain mean to you?* In deep gratitude to my students. You are my wisest teachers always. In summary here are a few of their answers:

> My intuitive mountain means that I am not afraid to visit the deep dark places. To lean into my pain and discover what actually lies there. The why? The fear.., the things that have held me back. Right now I feel like Kali is speaking to me and cheering me on.
>
> Take time. Breathe. Listen.
> Go within. Grounded. Reflect. True North.
>
> Letting go of control. Trusting in the universe more, trusting in myself more, breathing and being silent more so I can hear what my intuition is saying to me. Being peaceful. Grace.
>
> Honouring my authentic and best self.
>
> It means TRUSTING MYSELF, being strong, firm and I wavering. There is an internal and external depth and working at all times! We are all Interconnected, and connected to each other! Space, Freedom, Light and Shadow, Moon and Sun, Heaven and Earth, Love and Fear.

It means sitting in integrity and knowing I am fully supported and loved.

Trust your gut, intuition and reduce the overthinking. Don't let fear stop you from doing things. Following your intuition and not worrying what others think!

Stepping forward boldly with courage and with a peaceful heart, knowing all will work out as it needs to, without the pushing or the struggling.

Honesty. Rawness. Sometimes hard work.

Connecting with your authentic self ... sometimes digging deep to even find her and other times making sure you follow her on where she wants to take you. Learning that letting go of expectations doesn't mean not being ambitious or being lazy... And that mountains are mighty, sometimes scary and that the aim is not to conquer the mountain but to relish it, respect it and let it show you its joyous wonders.

ACKNOWLEDGEMENTS

To my husband Oli—you are my solid mountain. Thank you for taking care of our home, cooking every dinner and driving every morning sport run so I can write and stay sane. Can't believe we've been together 24 years.

To my girls Leila and Zoë—you are my big little loves. Thank you for choosing me and reflecting back the truth I need to see every day.

To my editor Bella—thank you for your expert guidance, our conversations, the title of *big little,* your coaching and support that saw the potential in this story and encouraged me to keep writing the damn book. A powerful woman with the courage to cut right to the core. I'll be back.

To my publisher Natasha and the team at The Kind Press—after much seeking, I landed upon the perfect people who shared my vision and were so generous from the beginning. You made the whole process flow with ease and completely empathised with the author's needs. True professionals with heart.

To my spiritual director Ricci-Jane—your forward left me a little wordless. You have always been a safe place for me to land and I am drawn to your spiritual fierceness for good reason. Thank you for calling me out again and again when I want to hide. Thank you for being an incredible teacher and always pushing the limits of what's possible.

To my coach Kemi—you have redefined the word 'power' for me to include myself. For that I am eternally grateful. Thank you for listening, thank you for helping me not waste my white privilege, thank you for your kindness, thank you for showing me what equality actually means. I could go on but I know you have flowers to tend to! You are a pure delight.

To my mentor Elena—to be in your presence helps me breathe easier. Thank you for showing me the importance of acceptance, death, love, and relationships. My feet are walking behind yours while

I learn more and more that every moment is a spiritual practice.

To Chelle and Tuuli—for being brave and sharing your sister stories. I know you will both keep writing and can't wait to read more. I am very grateful.

To Hayley—to say you're my partner in the soul wander retreat business diminishes what you really mean to me. Thank you for making the dream of travel possible so we can create these experiences that have formed so many of these stories. The movement grows.

To Hannah—for being the creative artist and designing the brilliant cover and illustrations. You bring the vision to life and am so grateful for the ten years we have partnered together.

To Prue—for capturing the photographs and coaching me to embody my 'why'. Your friendship and encouragement the last decade is invaluable.

To my inner circle, sister, my friends past and present—thank you for even calling me a friend when I come round once a year like a solar eclipse and forget to return phone calls.

To my mum—thank you for believing in my creative writing from the moment I learnt the alphabet. You kept every page in a box which I treasure.

To my breathwork, retreat, and yoga community—thank you for witnessing me tell stories week after week. It is a privilege to watch lifelong connections grow in this open space. We don't heal in isolation, but in community.

To the reader—thank you for making it to the very end. You have dared to face your vulnerability and recognised your charm. Keep breathing and coming back to the practices in this book.

To the goddesses, thank you.

To the authors who inspire me—Glennon Doyle, Elizabeth Gilbert and Cheryl Strayed. There are many more, however, as brilliant memoirists you are all trailblazers. You don't write books; you write life rafts for humanity to keep our heads above water so we can still breathe.

ABOUT THE AUTHOR

TINA BRUCE is a retreat leader, author, intuitive mentor, keynote speaker, rebirthing breathwork facilitator, yoga and meditation teacher and spinal energetics practitioner. Tina is enthusiastic about trauma-informed somatic practices and inspiring others to heal. Her first book, "Mother's Medicine: The Birth of My Intuition" is a memoir about her own healing journey. Tina is the founder of the 'Big Little Breath™ Retreat Leadership Program' for spiritful leaders, co-founder of Soul Wander Retreats and facilitates programs locally and internationally with integrity and cultural connection. Tina walks her talk to support you through transformation and to lead with true power.

Tina's purpose is to empower people to trust their intuition so they can step more confidently on their soul path and reclaim their whole authentic self.

TO DEEPEN THE BIG LITTLE BREATH™ JOURNEY

Join the next Big Little Breath™ Leadership Program
tinabruce.com.au/big-little-breath-retreat-leaderhsip-program

Follow Tina at @tinabrucesoul or visit her website
tinabruce.com.au for all sessions, classes, events and
speaking availability.

Wander over to @soulwanderretreats for full retreat details and to
register, visit the www.soulwanderretreats.com.au

For stories, meditations, truth telling and Tina's regular newsletter,
subscribe to tinabruce.substack.com

Milton Keynes UK
Ingram Content Group UK Ltd.
UKHW041053150824
446997UK00004B/160

9 780645 865691